MANGA MATH MYSTERIES

#3

THE SECRET GHOST

A Mystery with Distance and Measurement

by Melinda Thielbar

illustrated by Yuko Ota

GRAPHIC UNIVERSE™ • MINNEAPOLIS • NEW YORK

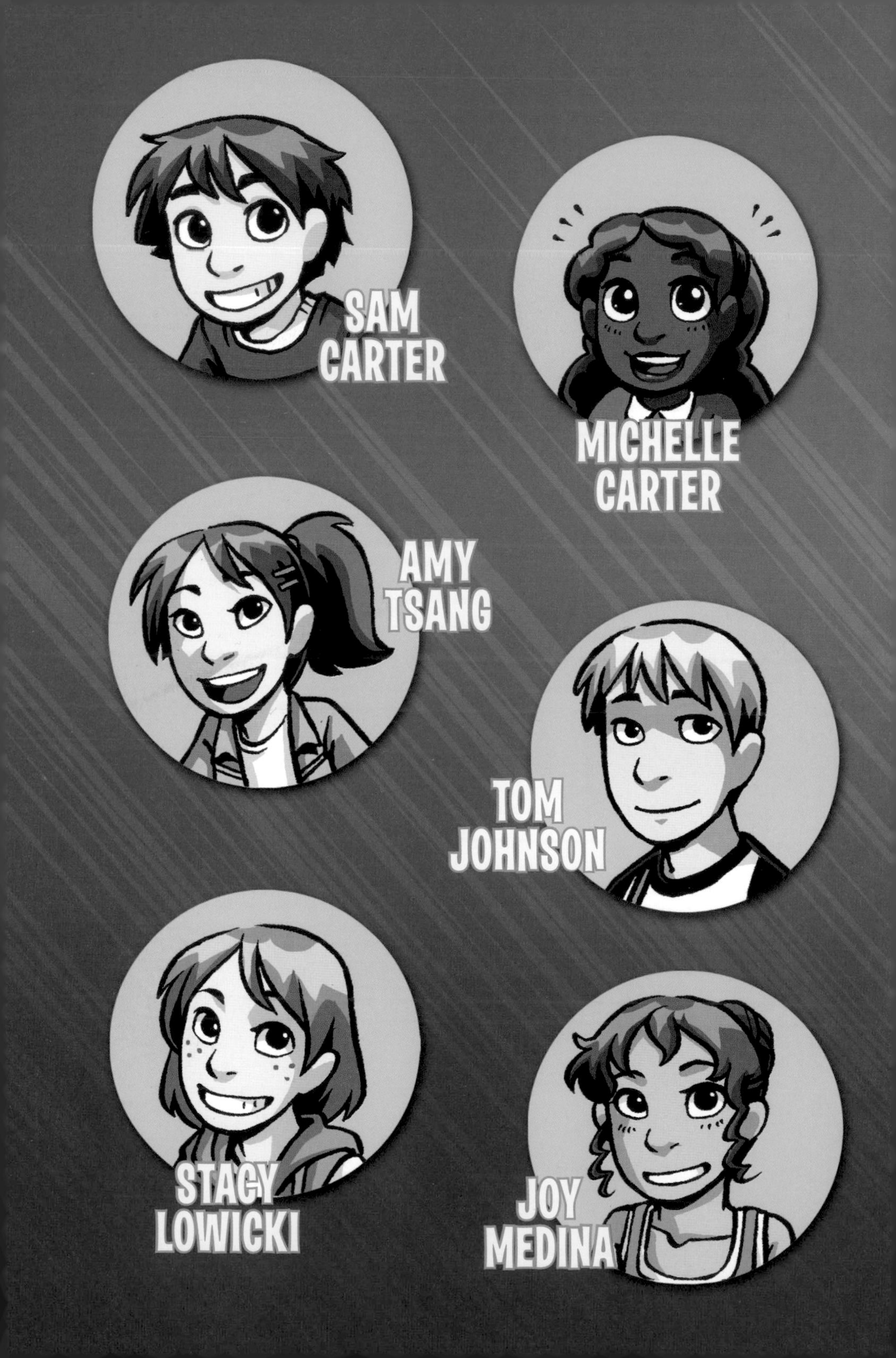
SAM CARTER
MICHELLE CARTER
AMY TSANG
TOM JOHNSON
STACY LOWICKI
JOY MEDINA

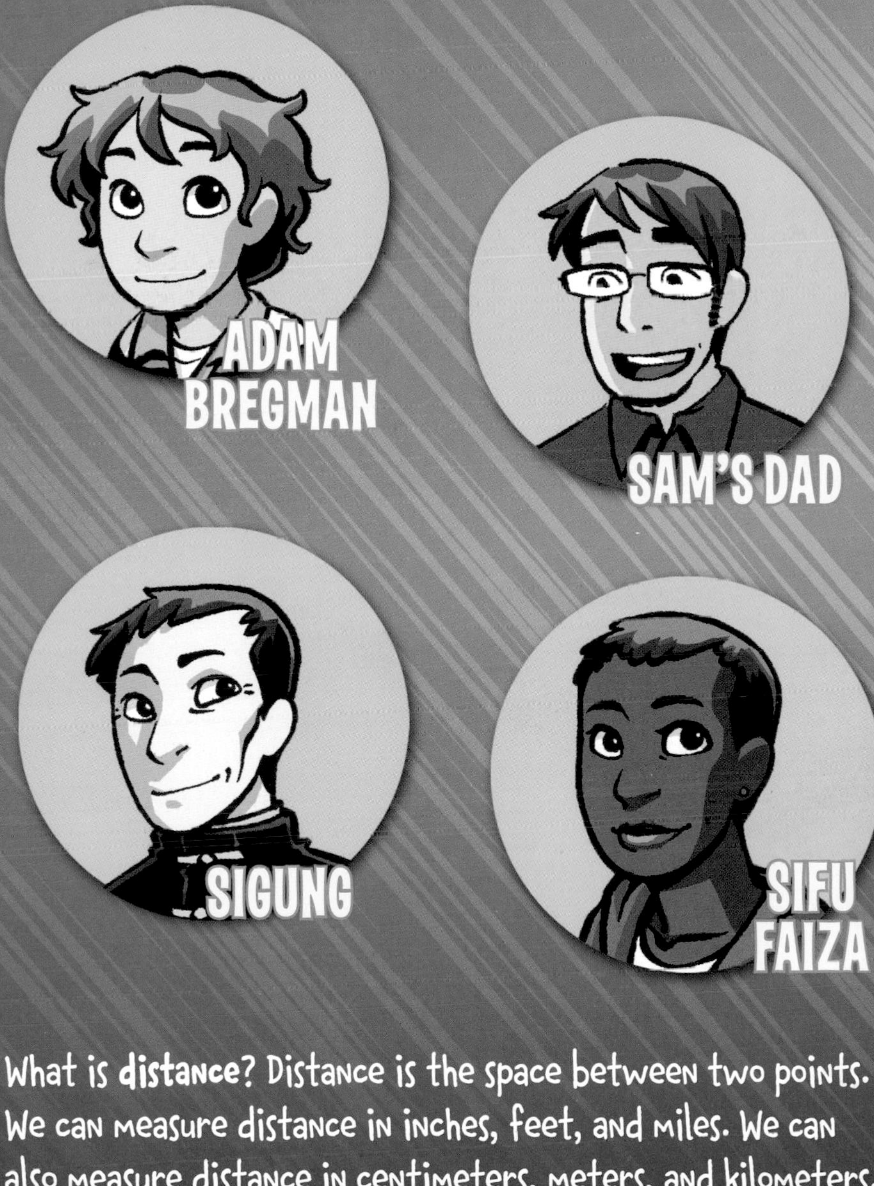
ADAM BREGMAN
SAM'S DAD
SIGUNG
SIFU FAIZA

What is **distance**? Distance is the space between two points. We can measure distance in inches, feet, and miles. We can also measure distance in centimeters, meters, and kilometers.

We **measure** to find out the length, size, or weight of something. We use **tools** to measure. We can measure distance with a **ruler** or a **yardstick** or a **tape measure**. Inches, feet, meters, and centimeters are called **units**. A unit can also be the length of your arm or how far you step when you walk.

Story by Melinda Thielbar
Pencils and inks by Yuko Ota
Coloring by Hi-Fi Design
Lettering by Marshall Dillon

Copyright © 2010 by Lerner Publishing Group, Inc.

Graphic Universe™ is a trademark of Lerner Publishing Group, Inc.

Graphic Universe™
A division of Lerner Publishing Group, Inc.
241 First Avenue North
Minneapolis, MN 55401 U.S.A.

Website address: www.lernerbooks.com

Library of Congress Cataloging-in-Publication Data

Thielbar, Melinda.
 The secret ghost : a mystery with distance and measurement / story by Melinda Thielbar ; art by Yuko Ota.
  p. cm. — (Manga math mysteries)
  Summary: Sam and his friends at the kung fu school use their understanding of width, length, circumference, and volume to uncover the secret of the noises behind the walls of a big Victorian house.
  ISBN: 978–0–7613–3855–0 (lib. bdg. : alk. paper)
  1. Graphic novels. [1. Graphic novels. 2. Mystery and detective stories. 3. Measurement—Fiction. 4. Mathematics—Fiction. 5. Kung fu—Fiction. 6. Haunted houses—Fiction.] I. Ota, Yuko, ill. II. Title.
PZ7.7.T48Se 2010
741.5'973—dc22   2008053243

Manufactured in the United States of America
1 2 3 4 5 6 – DP – 15 14 13 12 11 10

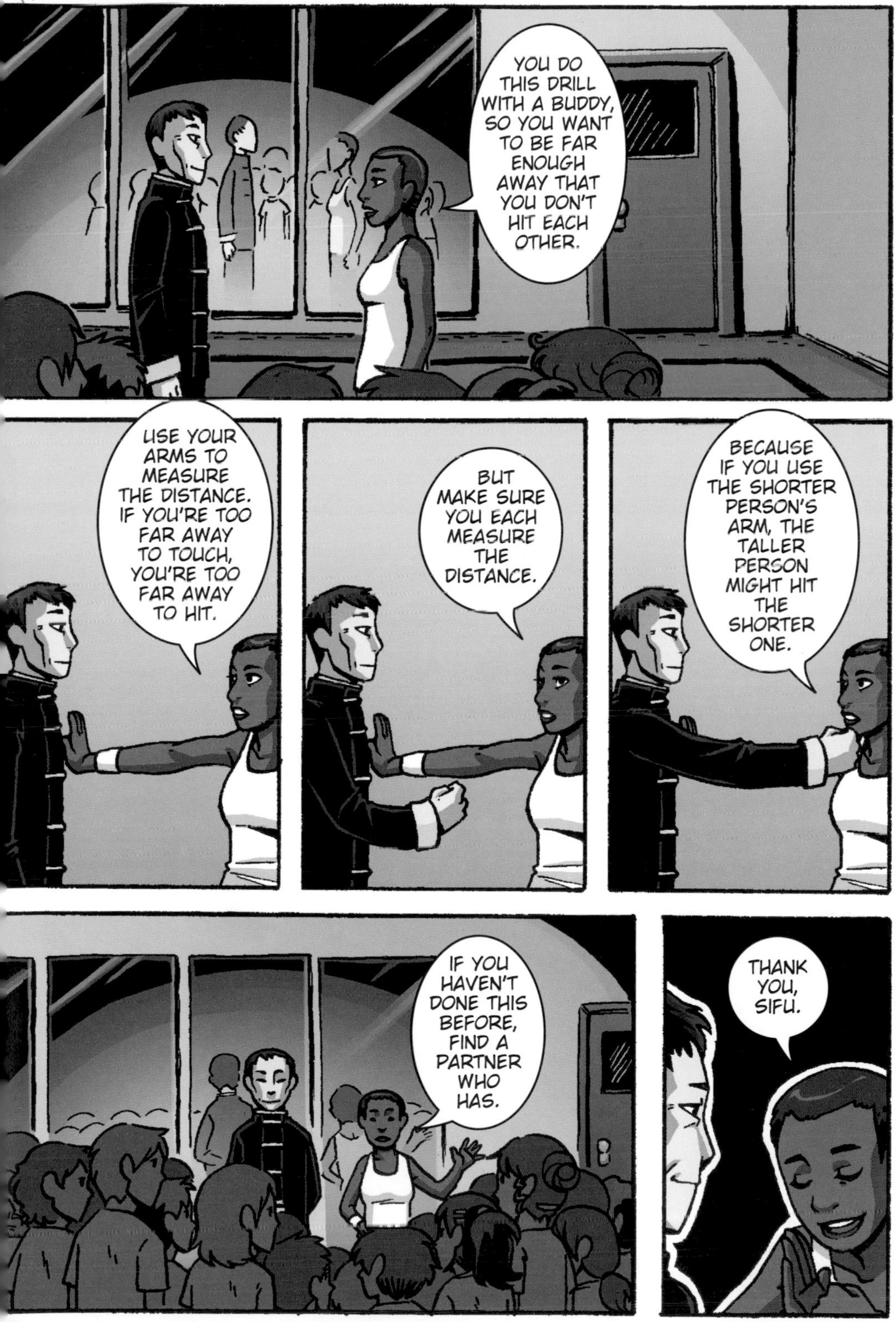
YOU DO THIS DRILL WITH A BUDDY, SO YOU WANT TO BE FAR ENOUGH AWAY THAT YOU DON'T HIT EACH OTHER.
USE YOUR ARMS TO MEASURE THE DISTANCE. IF YOU'RE TOO FAR AWAY TO TOUCH, YOU'RE TOO FAR AWAY TO HIT.
BUT MAKE SURE YOU EACH MEASURE THE DISTANCE.
BECAUSE IF YOU USE THE SHORTER PERSON'S ARM, THE TALLER PERSON MIGHT HIT THE SHORTER ONE.
IF YOU HAVEN'T DONE THIS BEFORE, FIND A PARTNER WHO HAS.
THANK YOU, SIFU.

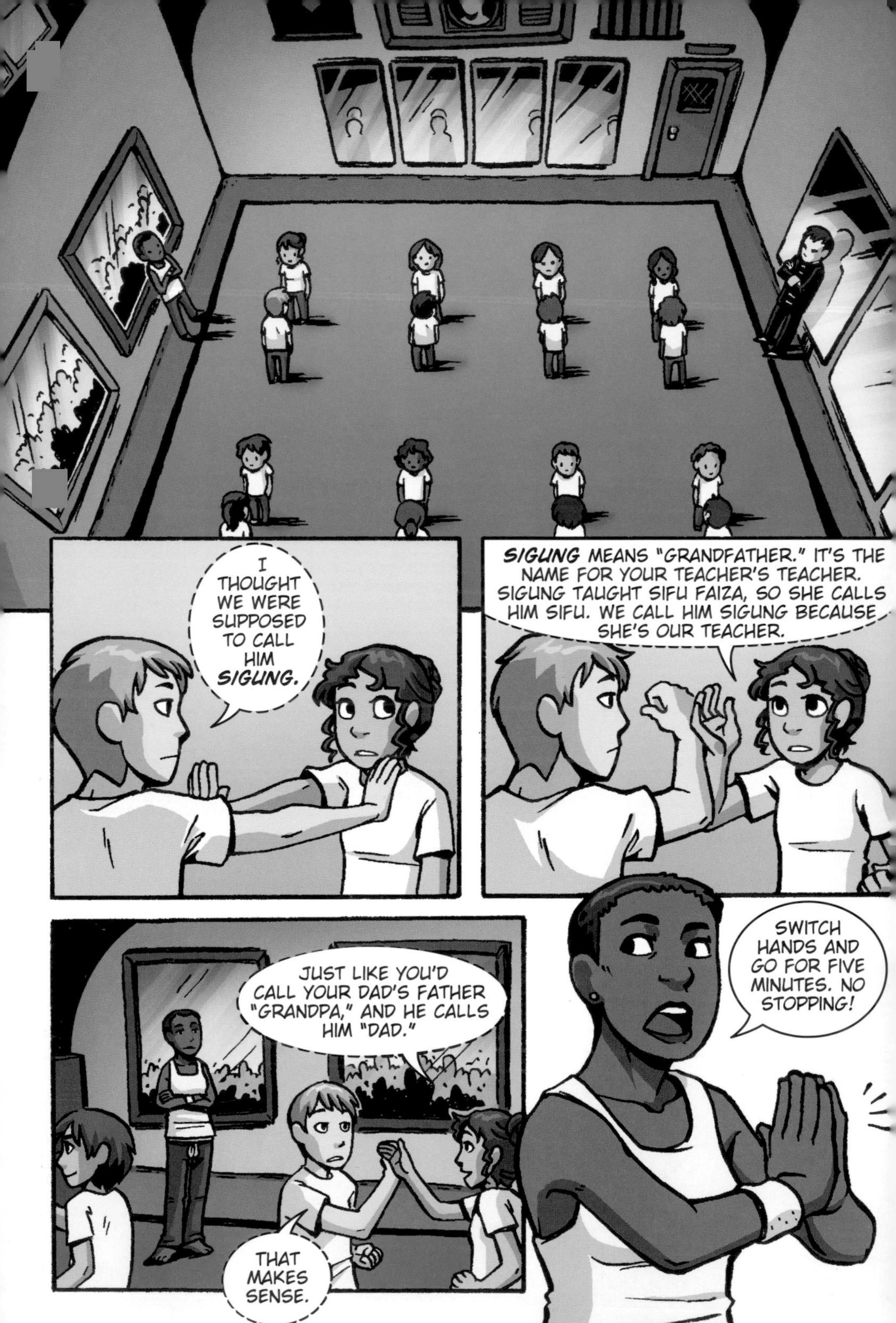
I THOUGHT WE WERE SUPPOSED TO CALL HIM *SIGUNG*.
SIGUNG MEANS "GRANDFATHER." IT'S THE NAME FOR YOUR TEACHER'S TEACHER. SIGUNG TAUGHT SIFU FAIZA, SO SHE CALLS HIM SIFU. WE CALL HIM SIGUNG BECAUSE SHE'S OUR TEACHER.
JUST LIKE YOU'D CALL YOUR DAD'S FATHER "GRANDPA," AND HE CALLS HIM "DAD."
THAT MAKES SENSE.
SWITCH HANDS AND GO FOR FIVE MINUTES. NO STOPPING!

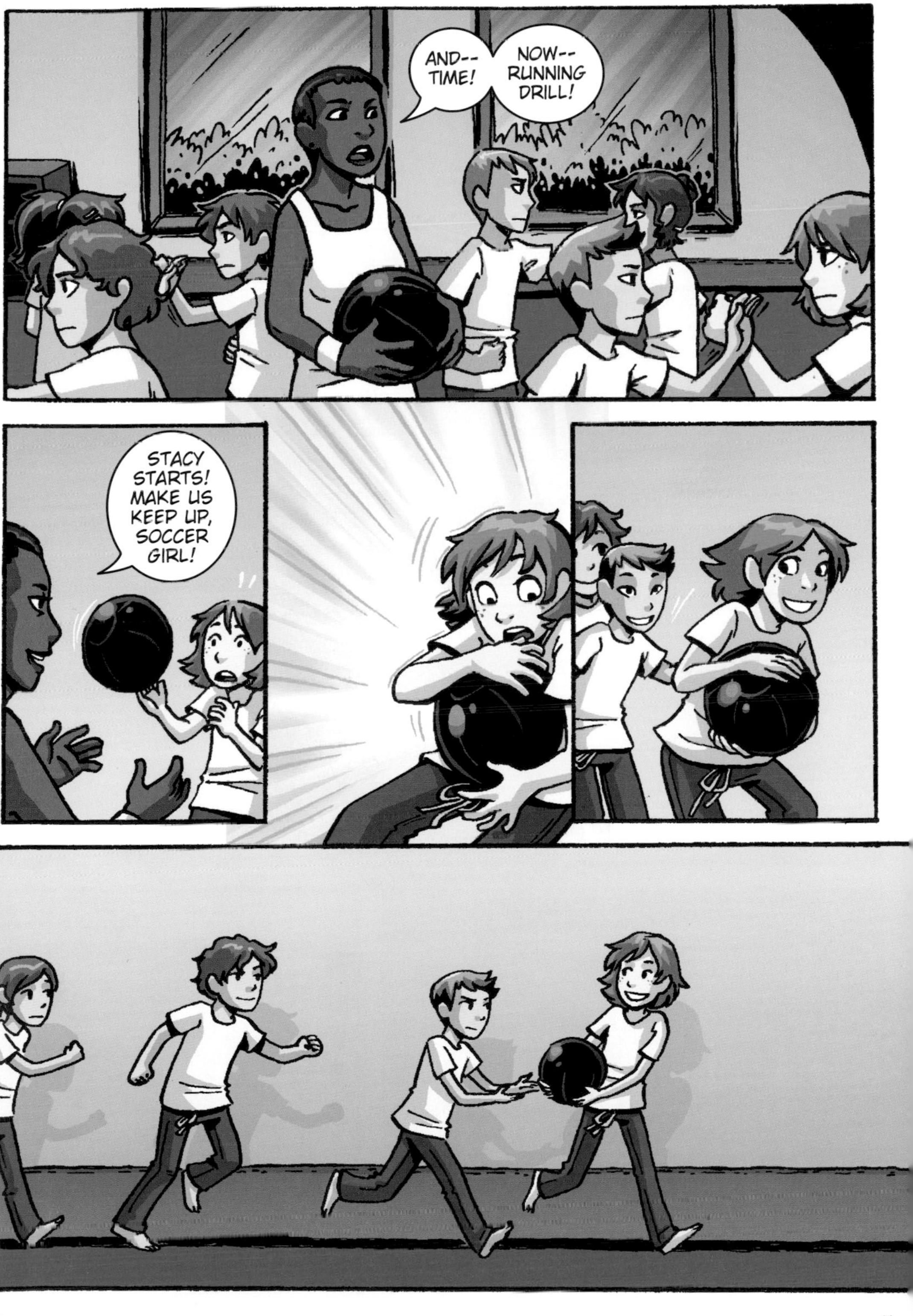
AND--
TIME!
NOW--
RUNNING
DRILL!
STACY
STARTS!
MAKE US
KEEP UP,
SOCCER
GIRL!

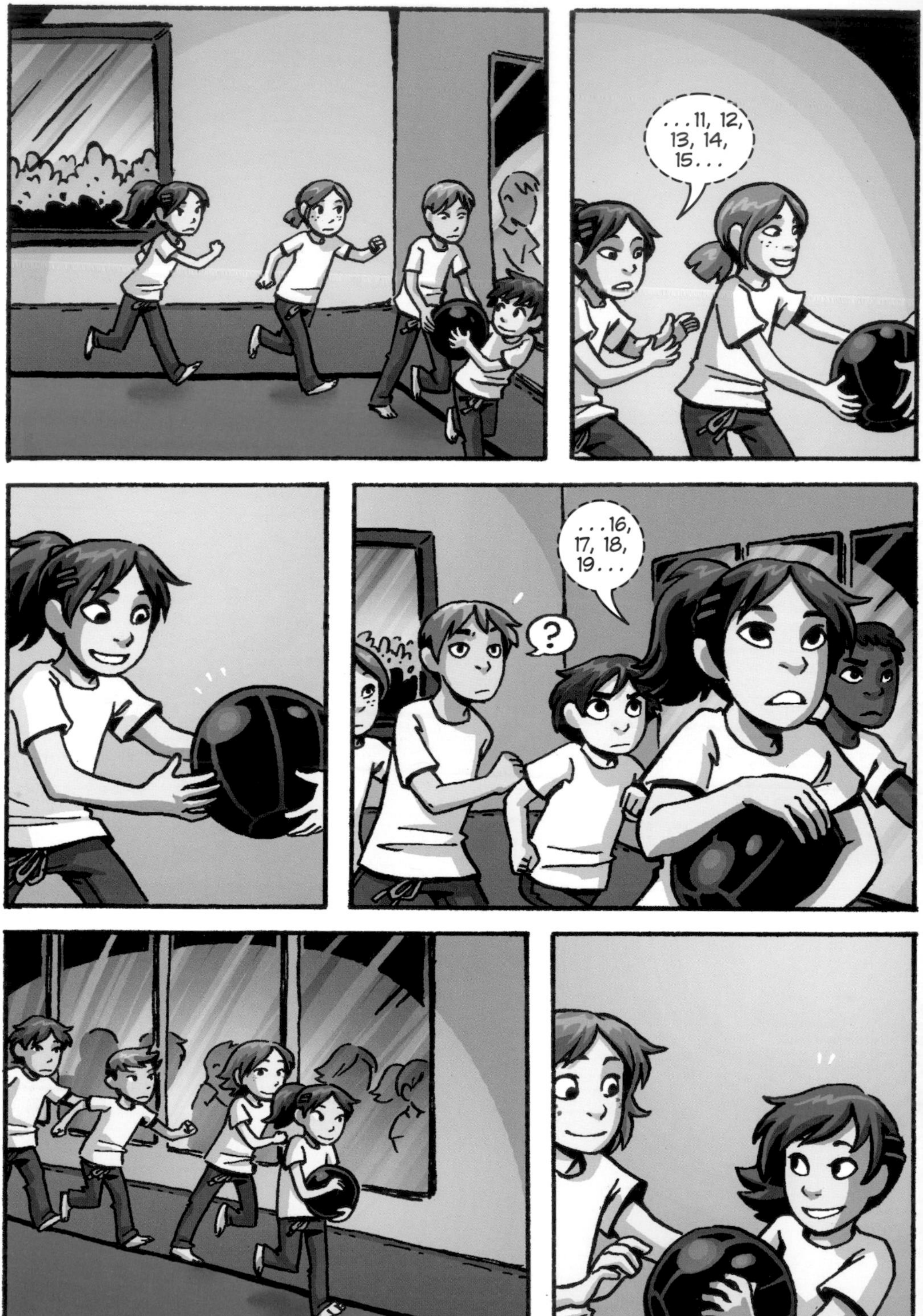
. . .11, 12, 13, 14, 15. . .
. . .16, 17, 18, 19. . .
?

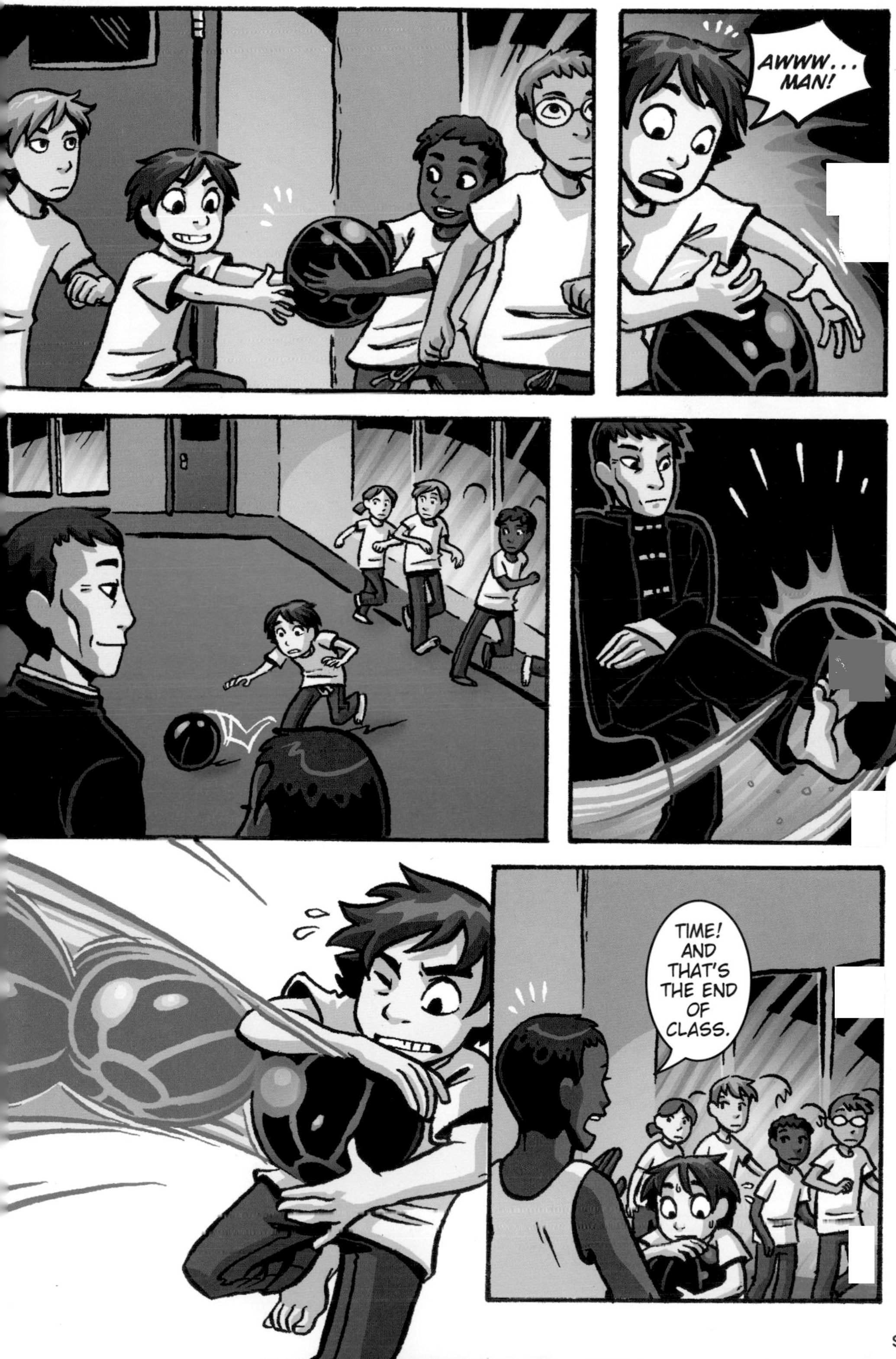
AWWW... MAN!
TIME! AND THAT'S THE END OF CLASS.

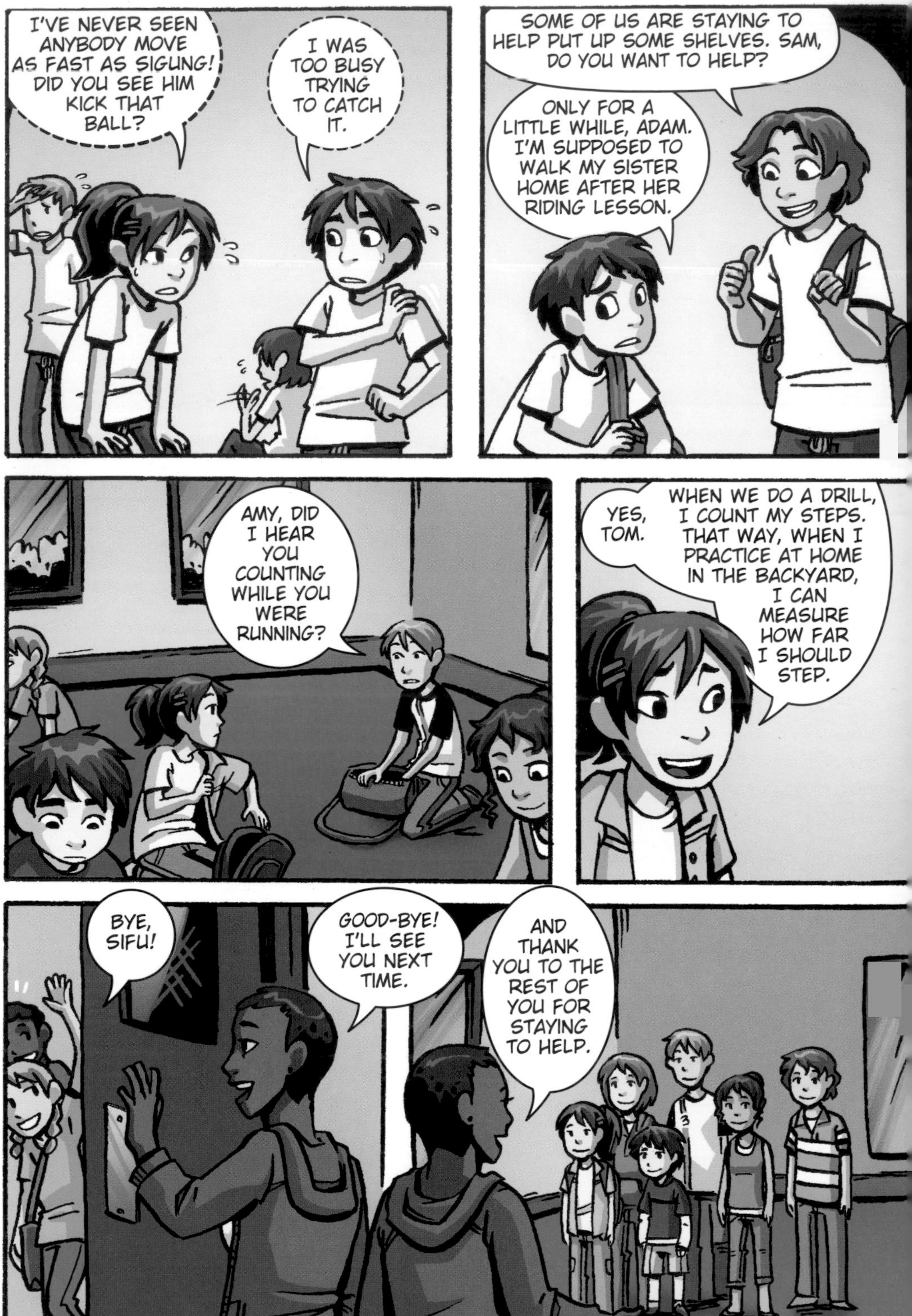
I'VE NEVER SEEN ANYBODY MOVE AS FAST AS SIGUNG! DID YOU SEE HIM KICK THAT BALL?
I WAS TOO BUSY TRYING TO CATCH IT.
SOME OF US ARE STAYING TO HELP PUT UP SOME SHELVES. SAM, DO YOU WANT TO HELP?
ONLY FOR A LITTLE WHILE, ADAM. I'M SUPPOSED TO WALK MY SISTER HOME AFTER HER RIDING LESSON.
AMY, DID I HEAR YOU COUNTING WHILE YOU WERE RUNNING?
YES, TOM.
WHEN WE DO A DRILL, I COUNT MY STEPS. THAT WAY, WHEN I PRACTICE AT HOME IN THE BACKYARD, I CAN MEASURE HOW FAR I SHOULD STEP.
BYE, SIFU!
GOOD-BYE! I'LL SEE YOU NEXT TIME.
AND THANK YOU TO THE REST OF YOU FOR STAYING TO HELP.

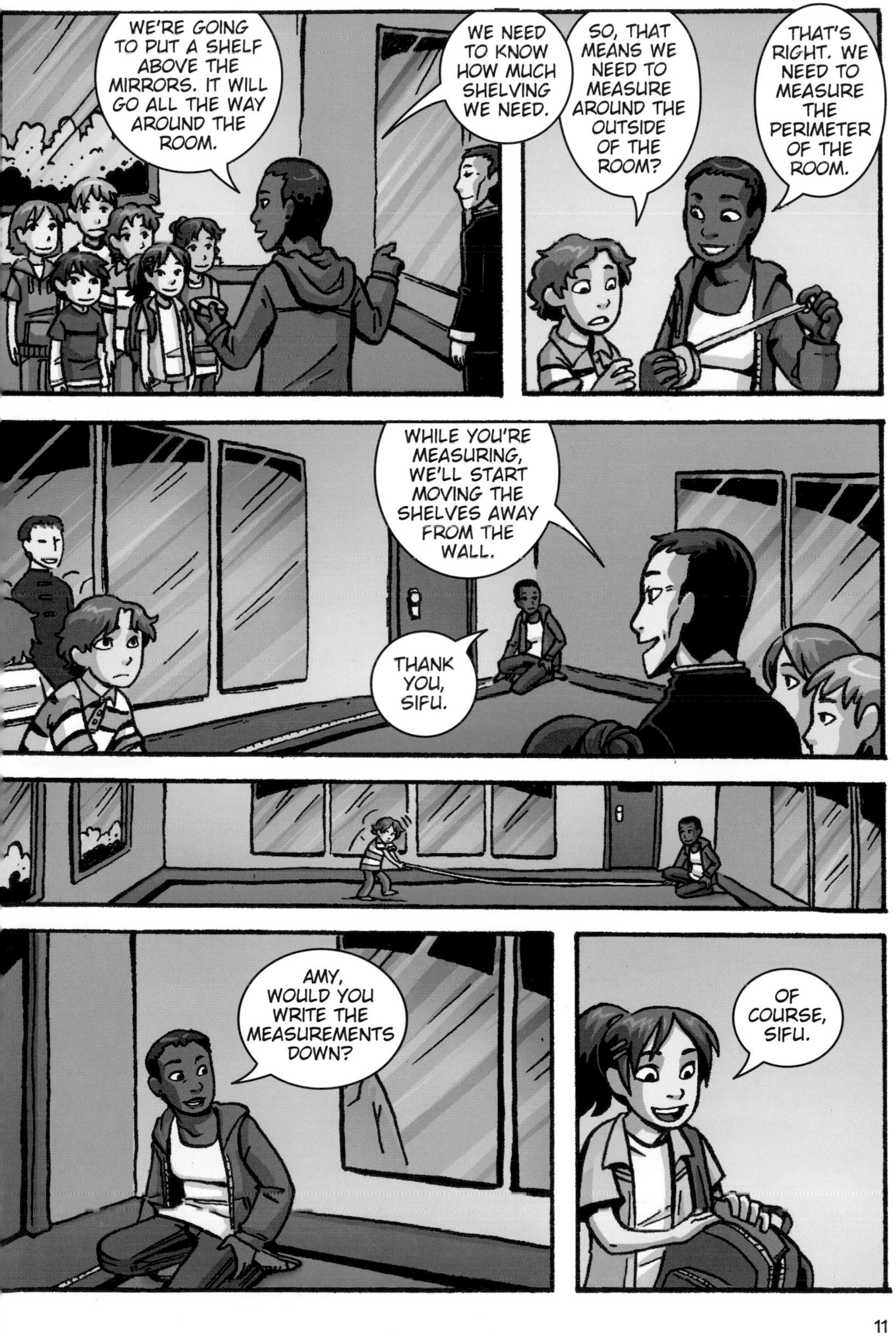
WE'RE GOING TO PUT A SHELF ABOVE THE MIRRORS. IT WILL GO ALL THE WAY AROUND THE ROOM.
WE NEED TO KNOW HOW MUCH SHELVING WE NEED.
SO, THAT MEANS WE NEED TO MEASURE AROUND THE OUTSIDE OF THE ROOM?
THAT'S RIGHT. WE NEED TO MEASURE THE PERIMETER OF THE ROOM.
WHILE YOU'RE MEASURING, WE'LL START MOVING THE SHELVES AWAY FROM THE WALL.
THANK YOU, SIFU.
AMY, WOULD YOU WRITE THE MEASUREMENTS DOWN?
OF COURSE, SIFU.

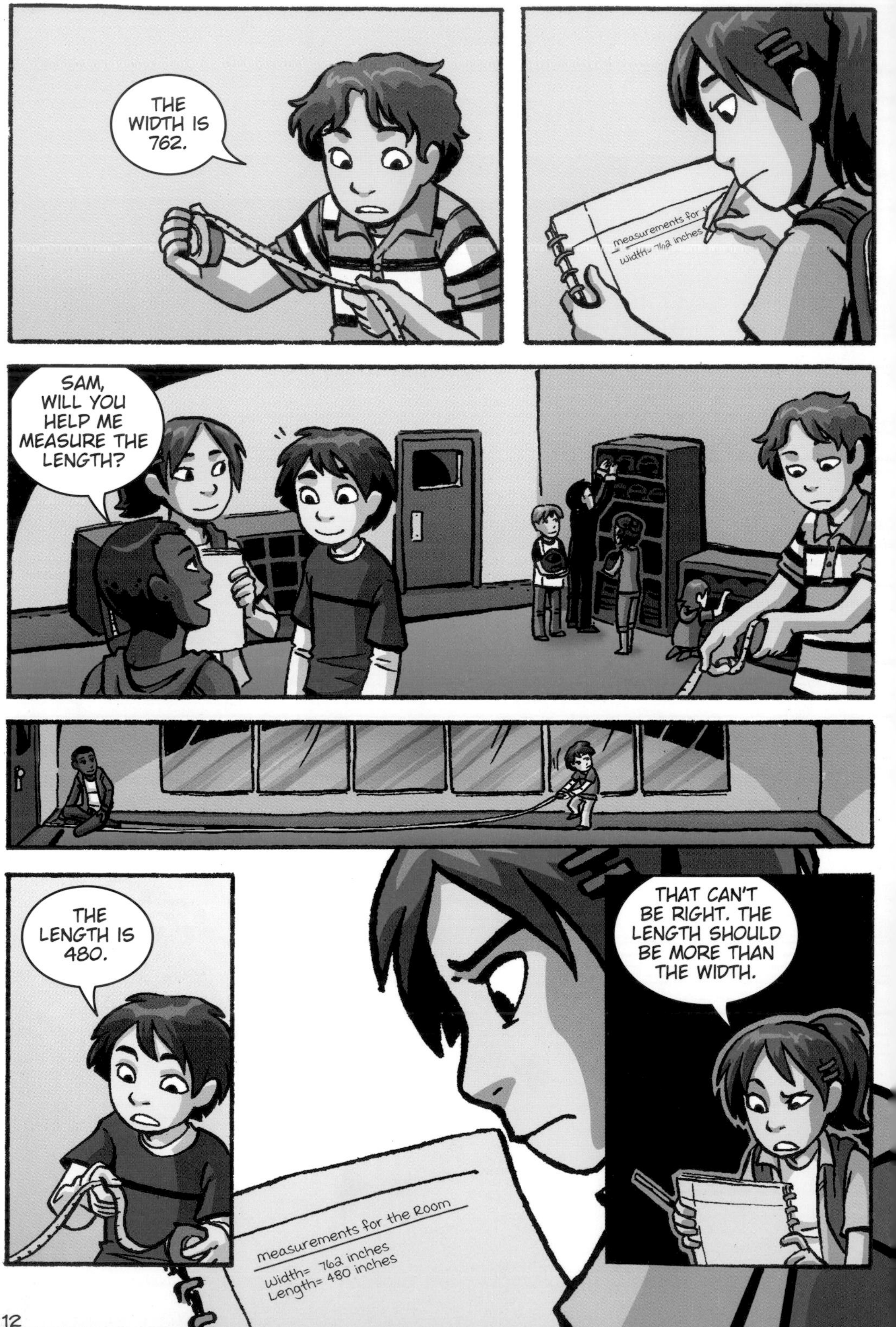
THE WIDTH IS 762.
measurements for th
Width= 762 inches
SAM, WILL YOU HELP ME MEASURE THE LENGTH?
THE LENGTH IS 480.
THAT CAN'T BE RIGHT. THE LENGTH SHOULD BE MORE THAN THE WIDTH.
measurements for the Room
Width= 762 inches
Length= 480 inches

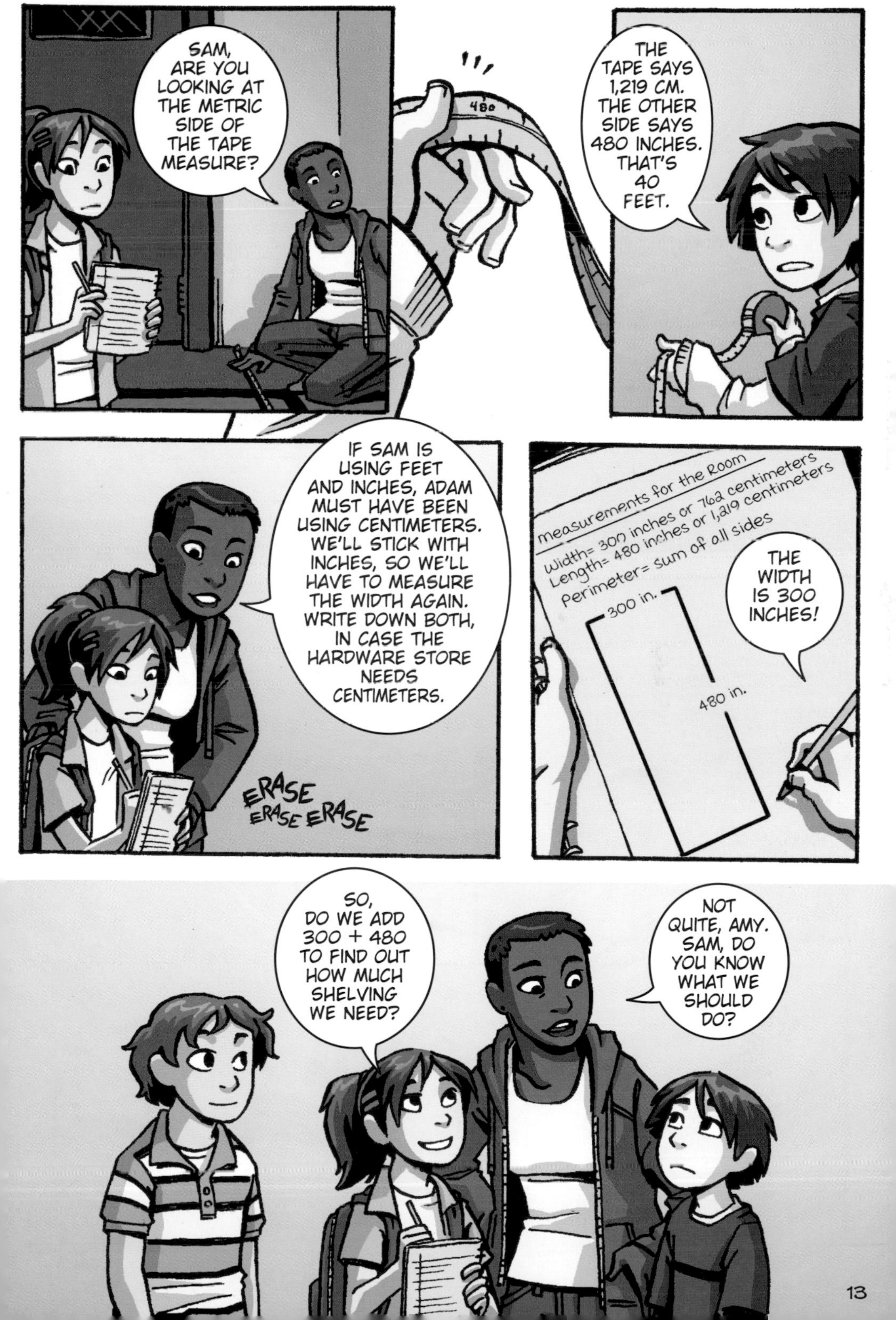
SAM, ARE YOU LOOKING AT THE METRIC SIDE OF THE TAPE MEASURE?
480
THE TAPE SAYS 1,219 CM. THE OTHER SIDE SAYS 480 INCHES. THAT'S 40 FEET.
IF SAM IS USING FEET AND INCHES, ADAM MUST HAVE BEEN USING CENTIMETERS. WE'LL STICK WITH INCHES, SO WE'LL HAVE TO MEASURE THE WIDTH AGAIN. WRITE DOWN BOTH, IN CASE THE HARDWARE STORE NEEDS CENTIMETERS.
ERASE ERASE ERASE
measurements for the Room
Width= 300 inches or 762 centimeters
Length= 480 inches or 1,219 centimeters
Perimeter= sum of all sides
300 in.
480 in.
THE WIDTH IS 300 INCHES!
SO, DO WE ADD 300 + 480 TO FIND OUT HOW MUCH SHELVING WE NEED?
NOT QUITE, AMY. SAM, DO YOU KNOW WHAT WE SHOULD DO?

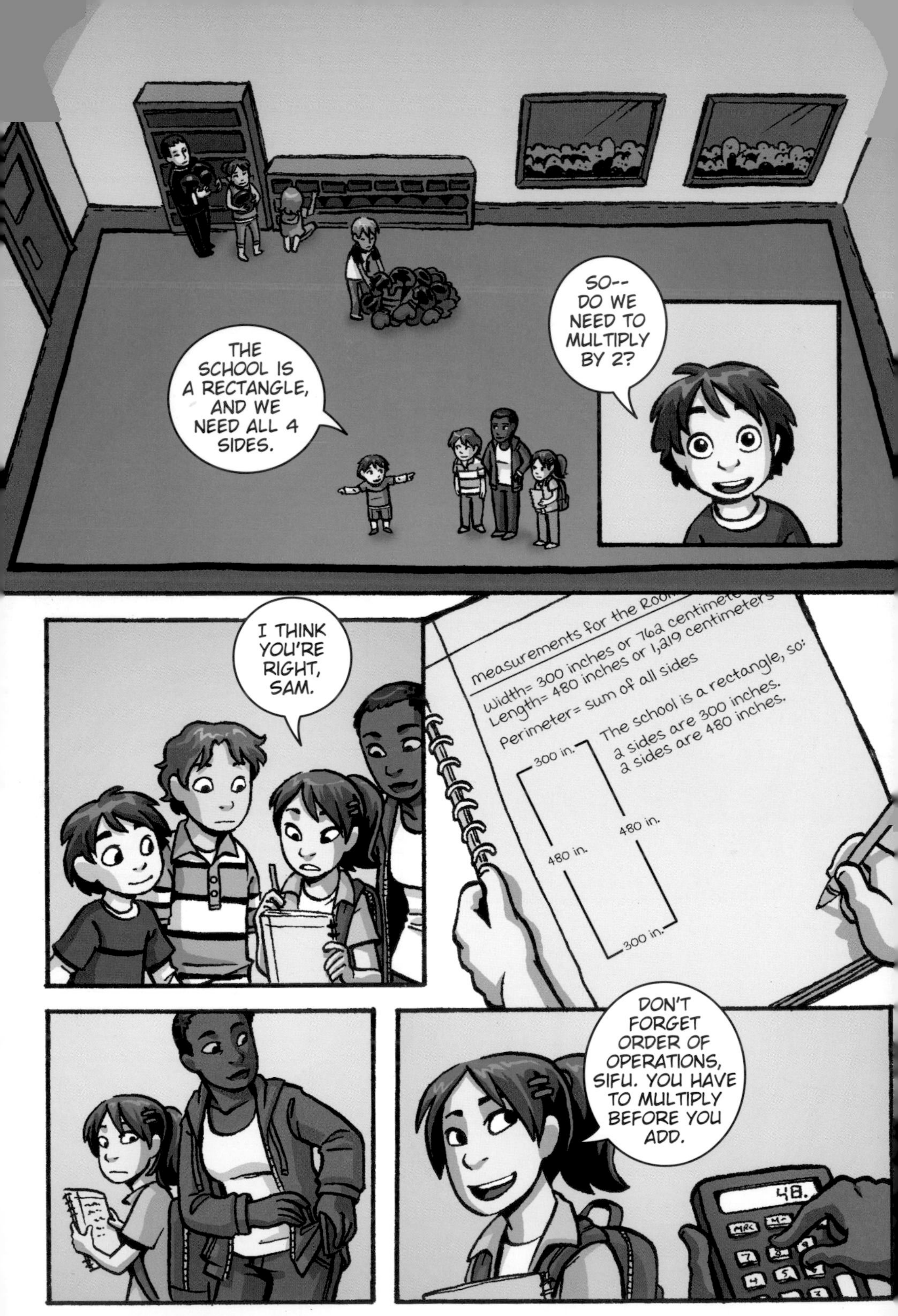
THE SCHOOL IS A RECTANGLE, AND WE NEED ALL 4 SIDES.
SO-- DO WE NEED TO MULTIPLY BY 2?
I THINK YOU'RE RIGHT, SAM.
measurements for the
Width= 300 inches or 762
Length= 480 inches or 1,219 centimeters
Perimeter= sum of all sides
The school is a rectangle, so:
2 sides are 300 inches.
2 sides are 480 inches.
300 in.
480 in.
480 in.
300 in.
DON'T FORGET ORDER OF OPERATIONS, SIFU. YOU HAVE TO MULTIPLY BEFORE YOU ADD.
48.

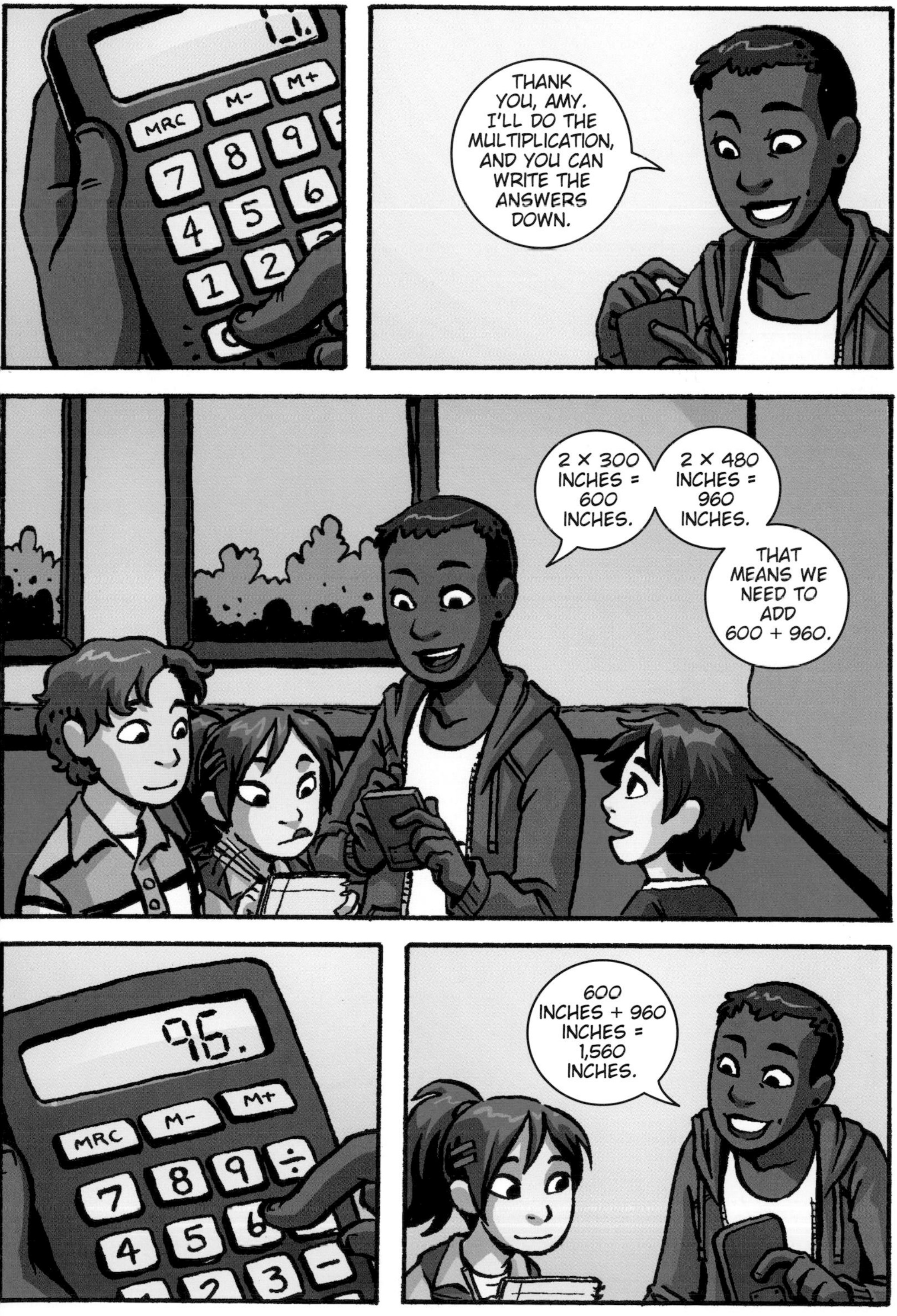
THANK YOU, AMY. I'LL DO THE MULTIPLICATION, AND YOU CAN WRITE THE ANSWERS DOWN.
2 × 300 INCHES = 600 INCHES.
2 × 480 INCHES = 960 INCHES.
THAT MEANS WE NEED TO ADD 600 + 960.
96.
600 INCHES + 960 INCHES = 1,560 INCHES.

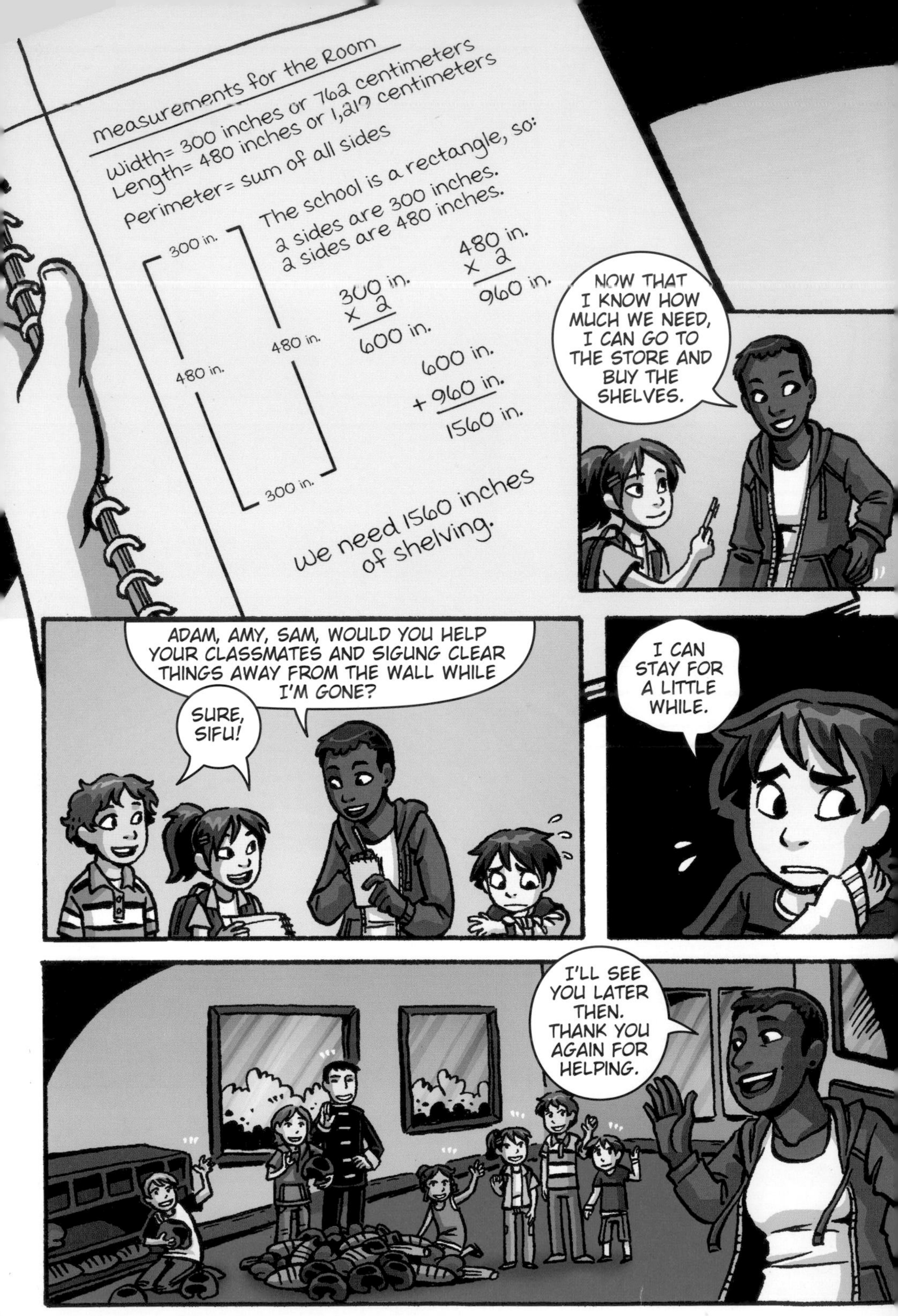
measurements for the Room
Width= 300 inches or 762 centimeters
Length= 480 inches or 1,219 centimeters
Perimeter= sum of all sides
The school is a rectangle, so:
2 sides are 300 inches.
2 sides are 480 inches.
300 in.
480 in.
480 in.
300 in.
300 in. x 2 = 600 in.
480 in. x 2 = 960 in.
600 in. + 960 in. = 1560 in.
We need 1560 inches of shelving.
NOW THAT I KNOW HOW MUCH WE NEED, I CAN GO TO THE STORE AND BUY THE SHELVES.
ADAM, AMY, SAM, WOULD YOU HELP YOUR CLASSMATES AND SIGUNG CLEAR THINGS AWAY FROM THE WALL WHILE I'M GONE?
SURE, SIFU!
I CAN STAY FOR A LITTLE WHILE.
I'LL SEE YOU LATER THEN. THANK YOU AGAIN FOR HELPING.

WHILE WE HAVE THIS STUFF OFF THE SHELVES, LET'S WIPE OFF THE DUST.

YES, SIGUNG.

YOU LOOK TIRED, SAM. IS EVERYTHING OK?

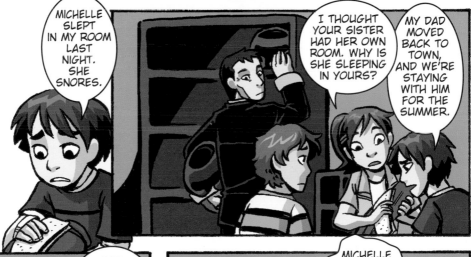

MICHELLE SLEPT IN MY ROOM LAST NIGHT. SHE SNORES.

I THOUGHT YOUR SISTER HAD HER OWN ROOM. WHY IS SHE SLEEPING IN YOURS?

MY DAD MOVED BACK TO TOWN, AND WE'RE STAYING WITH HIM FOR THE SUMMER.

DAD BOUGHT AN OLD HOUSE. IT MAKES ALL KINDS OF WEIRD SOUNDS AT NIGHT.

MICHELLE THINKS THERE'S A GHOST IN HER ROOM, SO SHE'S AFRAID TO SLEEP THERE.

DO YOU KNOW WHAT'S MAKING THE NOISES?

IT'S AN OLD HOUSE. IT JUST MAKES NOISE.

IF THE HOUSE IS MAKING LOUD NOISES, THERE MUST BE A REASON.

FAIZA TOLD ME YOU'VE SOLVED MYSTERIES BEFORE. MAYBE YOU CAN FIND OUT WHAT'S MAKING THE NOISES THAT SCARE YOUR SISTER.

YOU KNOW, THERE ARE ALL KINDS OF STORIES ABOUT SHAOLIN MONKS SOLVING MYSTERIES.

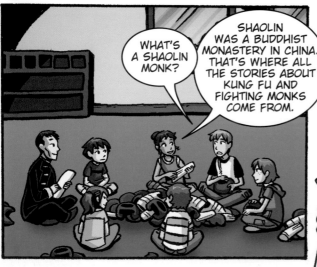

WHAT'S A SHAOLIN MONK?

SHAOLIN WAS A BUDDHIST MONASTERY IN CHINA. THAT'S WHERE ALL THE STORIES ABOUT KUNG FU AND FIGHTING MONKS COME FROM.

NOT *ALL* STORIES ABOUT KUNG FU ARE ABOUT SHAOLIN, BUT A LOT OF THEM ARE. THERE'S ONE THAT REMINDS ME OF YOUR PROBLEM, SAM.

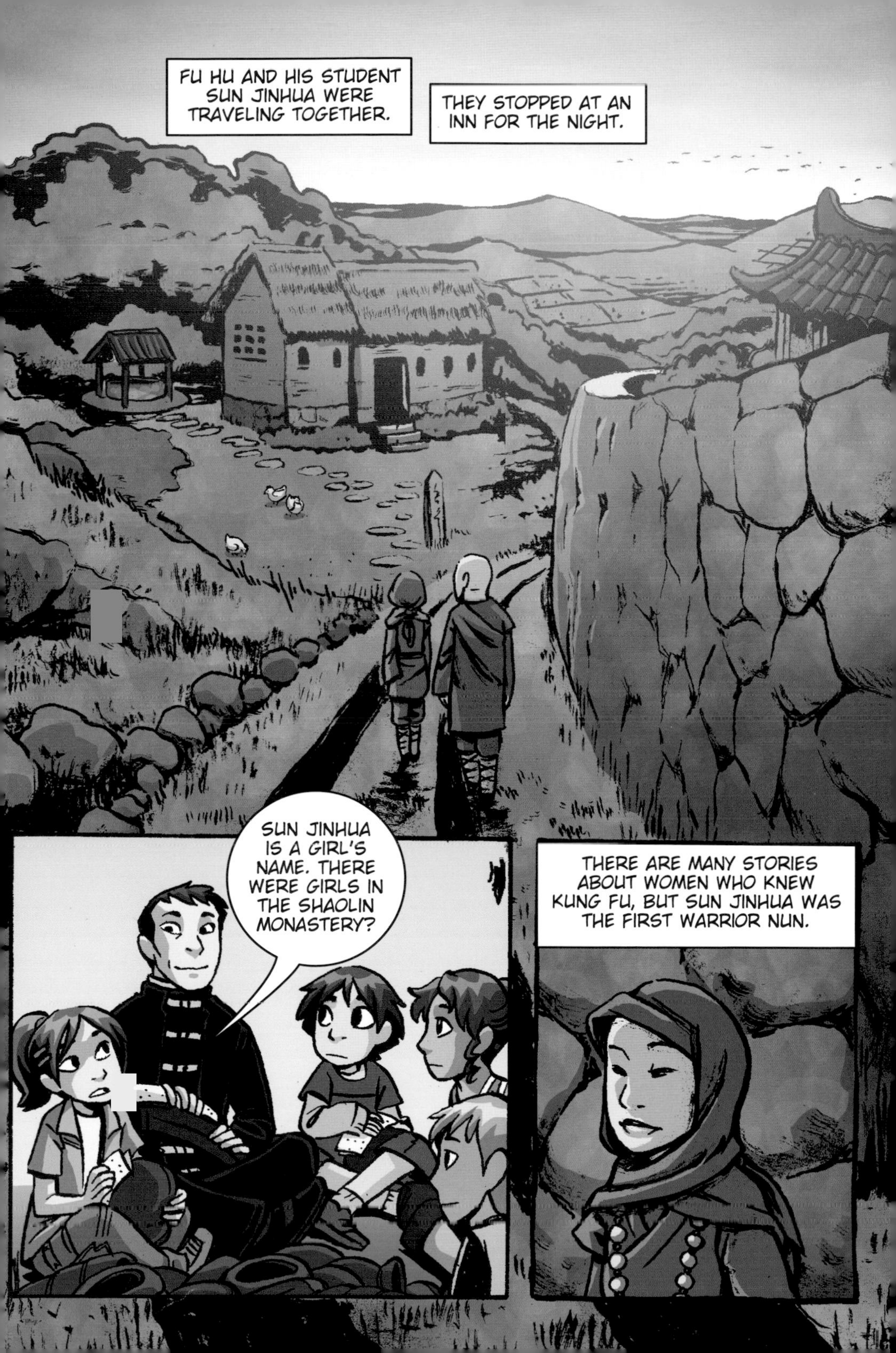
FU HU AND HIS STUDENT SUN JINHUA WERE TRAVELING TOGETHER.
THEY STOPPED AT AN INN FOR THE NIGHT.
SUN JINHUA IS A GIRL'S NAME. THERE WERE GIRLS IN THE SHAOLIN MONASTERY?
THERE ARE MANY STORIES ABOUT WOMEN WHO KNEW KUNG FU, BUT SUN JINHUA WAS THE FIRST WARRIOR NUN.

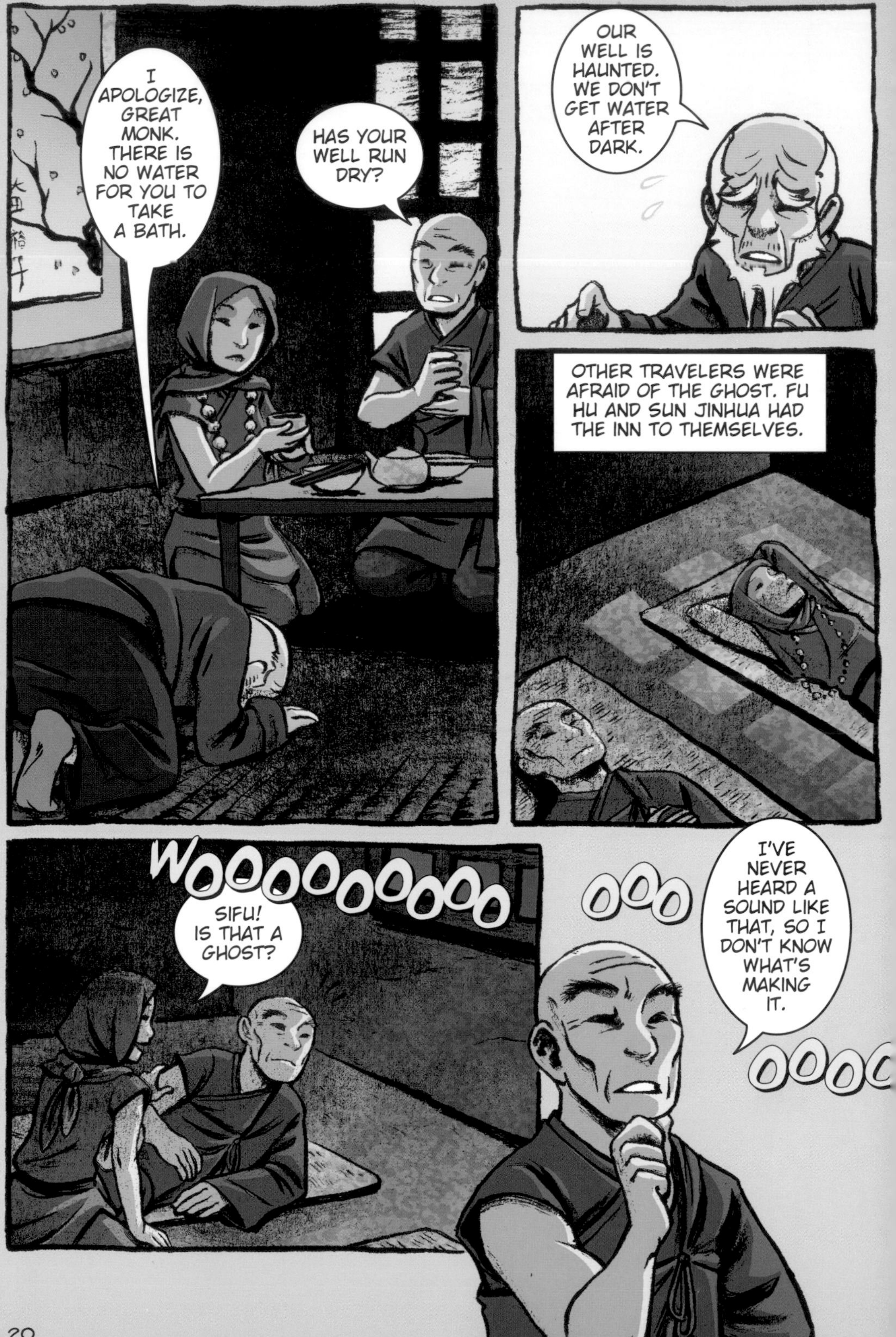
I APOLOGIZE, GREAT MONK. THERE IS NO WATER FOR YOU TO TAKE A BATH.
HAS YOUR WELL RUN DRY?
OUR WELL IS HAUNTED. WE DON'T GET WATER AFTER DARK.
OTHER TRAVELERS WERE AFRAID OF THE GHOST. FU HU AND SUN JINHUA HAD THE INN TO THEMSELVES.
WOOOOOOOOO
SIFU! IS THAT A GHOST?
OOO
I'VE NEVER HEARD A SOUND LIKE THAT, SO I DON'T KNOW WHAT'S MAKING IT.
OOOO

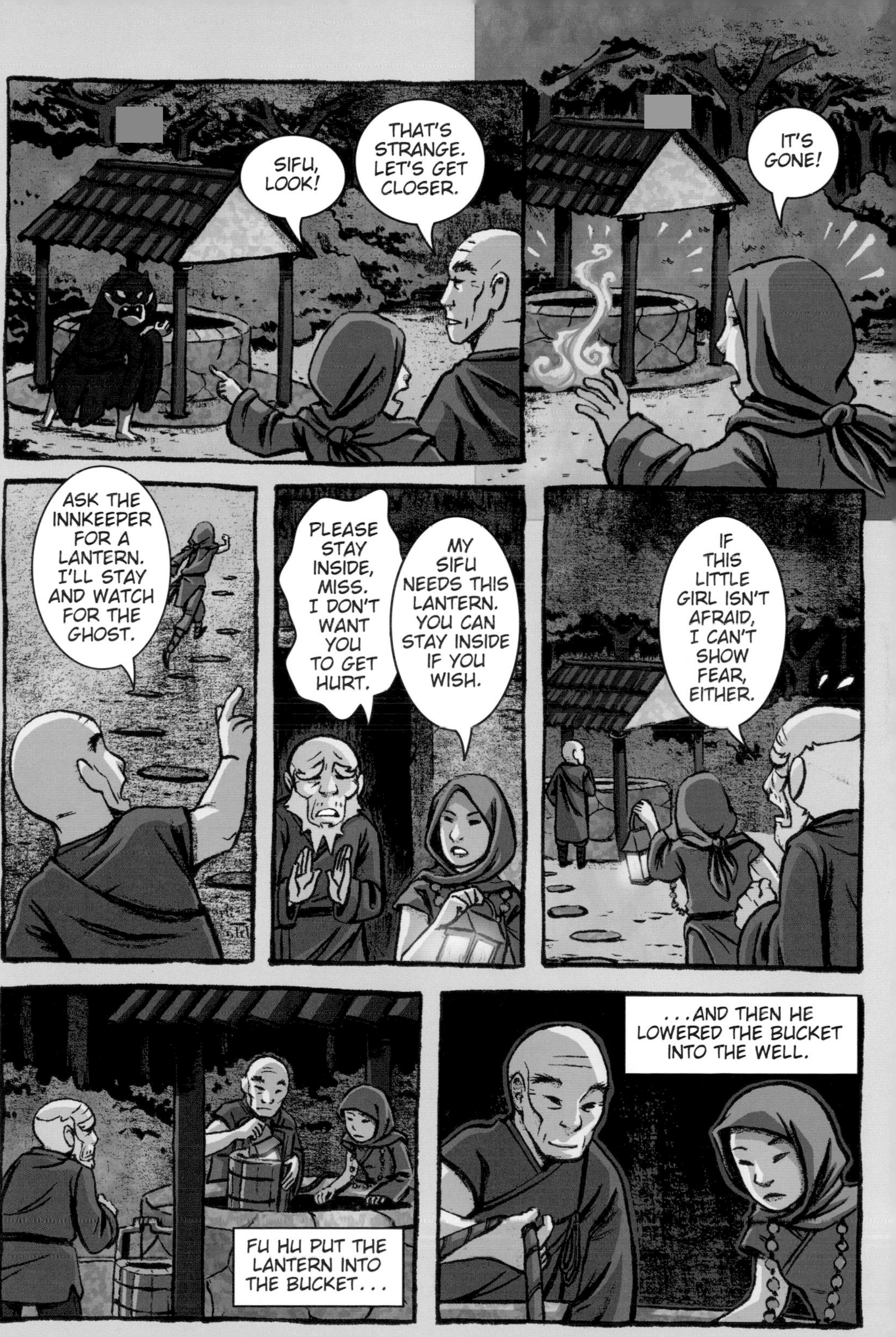
SIFU, LOOK!
THAT'S STRANGE. LET'S GET CLOSER.
IT'S GONE!
ASK THE INNKEEPER FOR A LANTERN. I'LL STAY AND WATCH FOR THE GHOST.
PLEASE STAY INSIDE, MISS. I DON'T WANT YOU TO GET HURT.
MY SIFU NEEDS THIS LANTERN. YOU CAN STAY INSIDE IF YOU WISH.
IF THIS LITTLE GIRL ISN'T AFRAID, I CAN'T SHOW FEAR, EITHER.
FU HU PUT THE LANTERN INTO THE BUCKET...
...AND THEN HE LOWERED THE BUCKET INTO THE WELL.

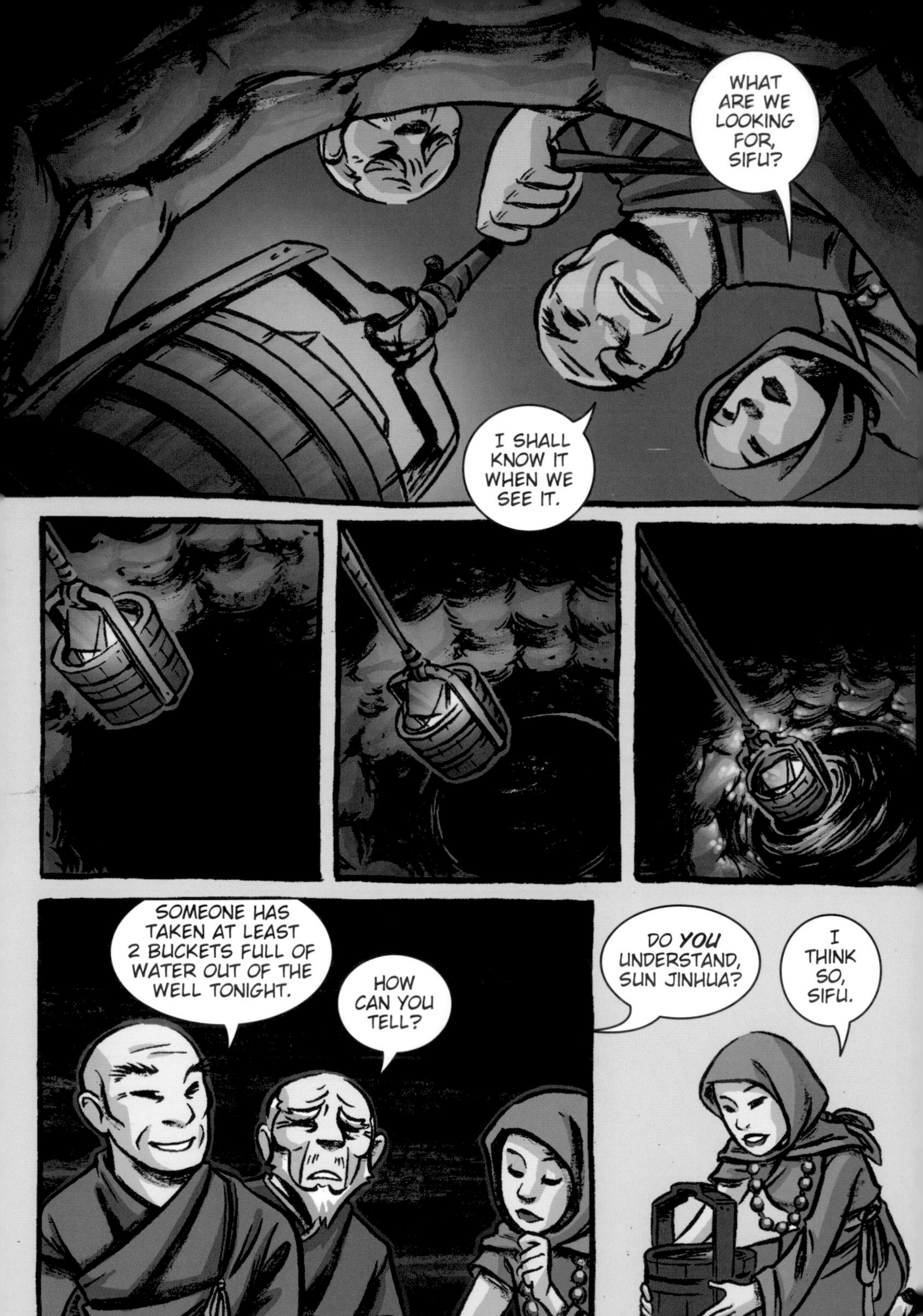
WHAT ARE WE LOOKING FOR, SIFU?
I SHALL KNOW IT WHEN WE SEE IT.
SOMEONE HAS TAKEN AT LEAST 2 BUCKETS FULL OF WATER OUT OF THE WELL TONIGHT.
HOW CAN YOU TELL?
DO *YOU* UNDERSTAND, SUN JINHUA?
I THINK SO, SIFU.

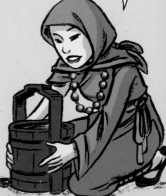

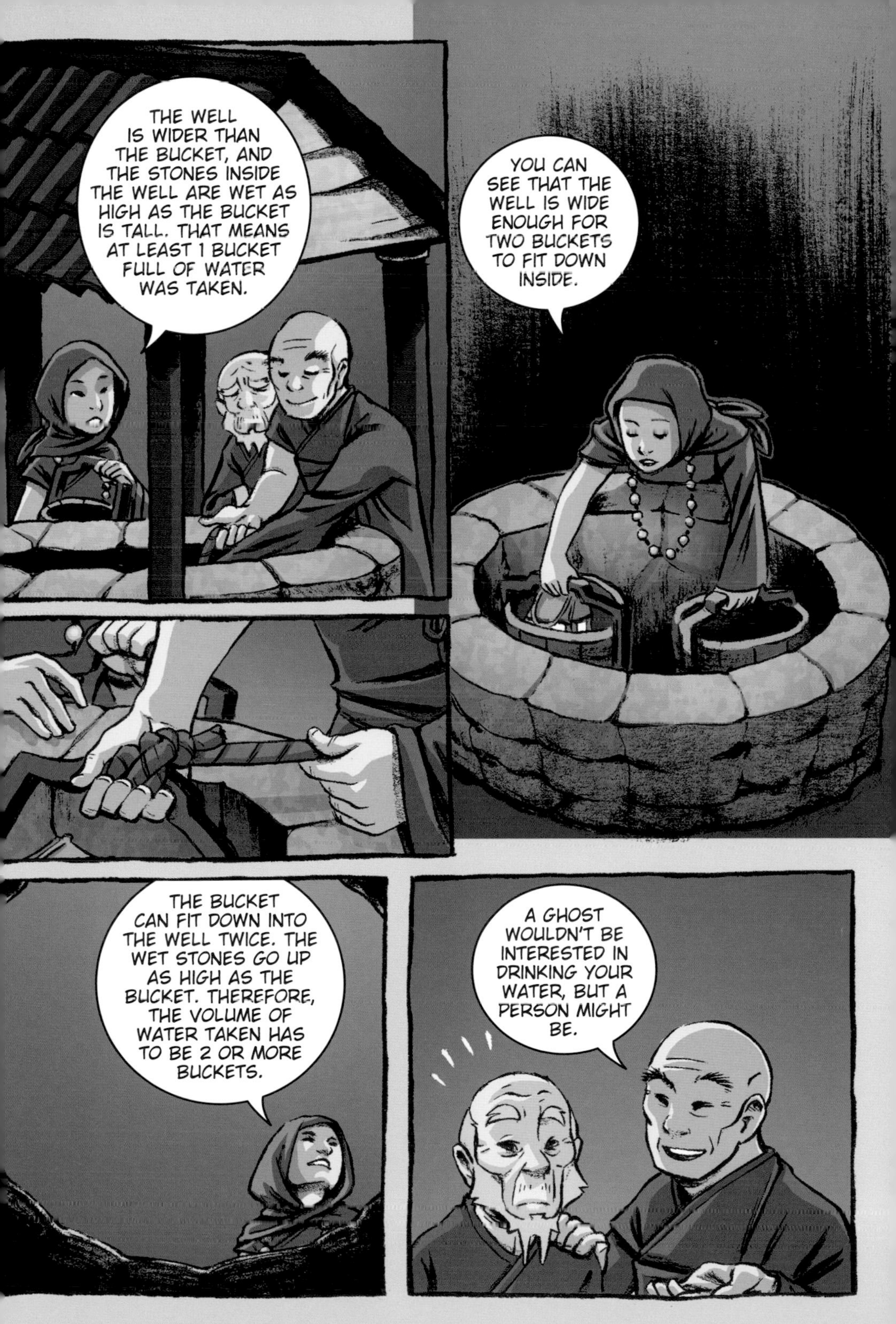
THE WELL IS WIDER THAN THE BUCKET, AND THE STONES INSIDE THE WELL ARE WET AS HIGH AS THE BUCKET IS TALL. THAT MEANS AT LEAST 1 BUCKET FULL OF WATER WAS TAKEN.
YOU CAN SEE THAT THE WELL IS WIDE ENOUGH FOR TWO BUCKETS TO FIT DOWN INSIDE.
THE BUCKET CAN FIT DOWN INTO THE WELL TWICE. THE WET STONES GO UP AS HIGH AS THE BUCKET. THEREFORE, THE VOLUME OF WATER TAKEN HAS TO BE 2 OR MORE BUCKETS.
A GHOST WOULDN'T BE INTERESTED IN DRINKING YOUR WATER, BUT A PERSON MIGHT BE.

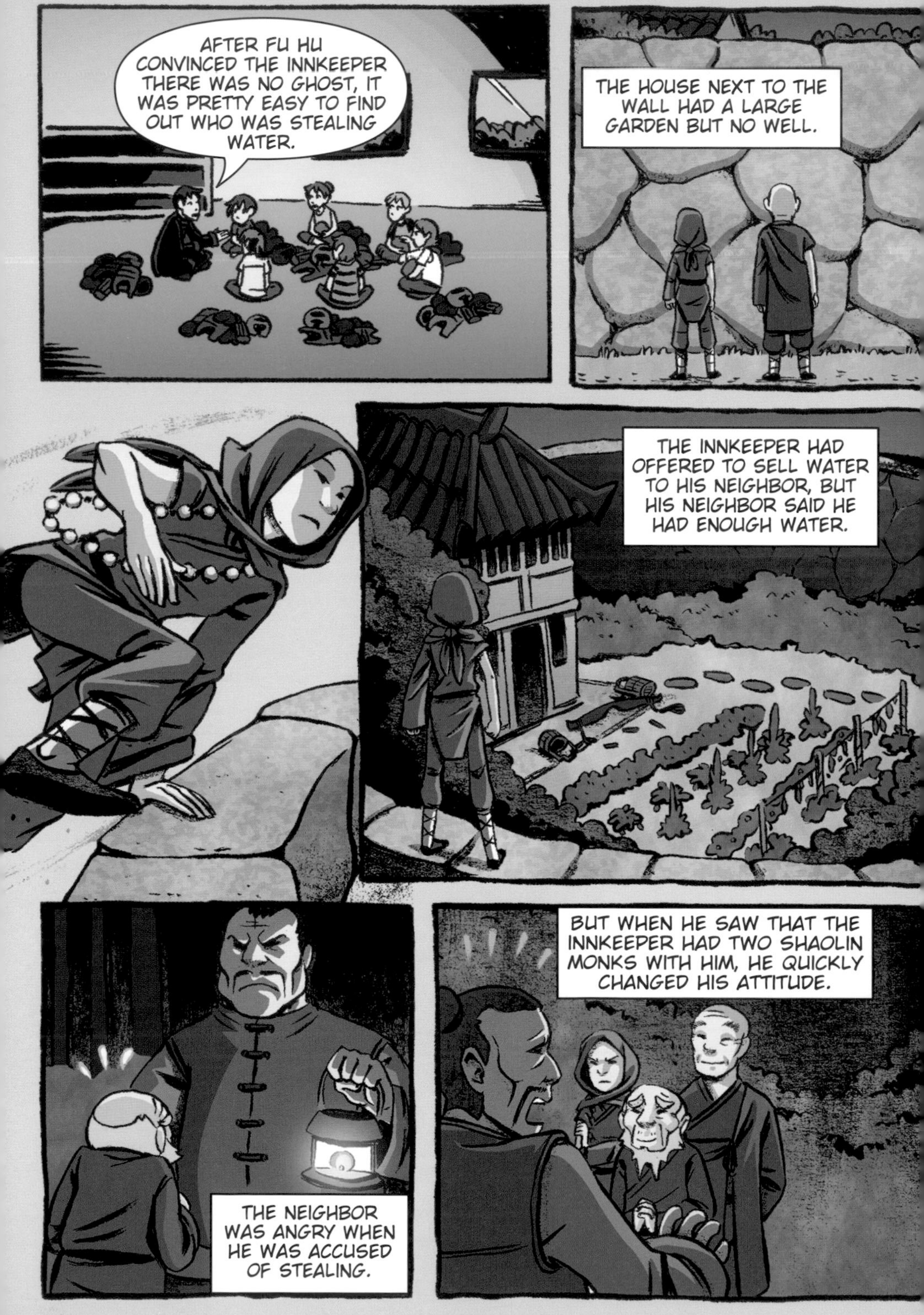
AFTER FU HU CONVINCED THE INNKEEPER THERE WAS NO GHOST, IT WAS PRETTY EASY TO FIND OUT WHO WAS STEALING WATER.
THE HOUSE NEXT TO THE WALL HAD A LARGE GARDEN BUT NO WELL.
THE INNKEEPER HAD OFFERED TO SELL WATER TO HIS NEIGHBOR, BUT HIS NEIGHBOR SAID HE HAD ENOUGH WATER.
THE NEIGHBOR WAS ANGRY WHEN HE WAS ACCUSED OF STEALING.
BUT WHEN HE SAW THAT THE INNKEEPER HAD TWO SHAOLIN MONKS WITH HIM, HE QUICKLY CHANGED HIS ATTITUDE.

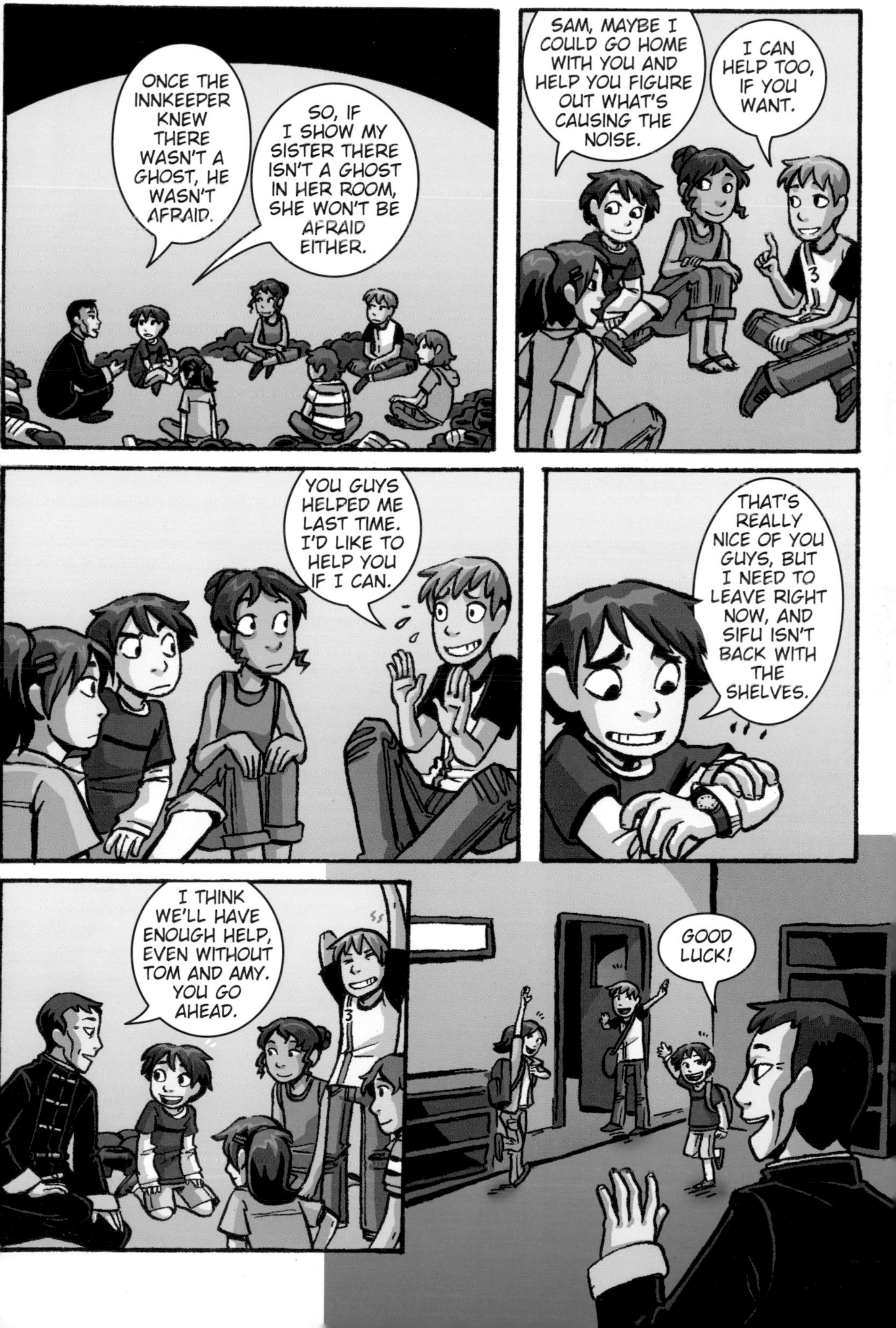

ONCE THE INNKEEPER KNEW THERE WASN'T A GHOST, HE WASN'T AFRAID.
SO, IF I SHOW MY SISTER THERE ISN'T A GHOST IN HER ROOM, SHE WON'T BE AFRAID EITHER.
SAM, MAYBE I COULD GO HOME WITH YOU AND HELP YOU FIGURE OUT WHAT'S CAUSING THE NOISE.
I CAN HELP TOO, IF YOU WANT.
YOU GUYS HELPED ME LAST TIME. I'D LIKE TO HELP YOU IF I CAN.
THAT'S REALLY NICE OF YOU GUYS, BUT I NEED TO LEAVE RIGHT NOW, AND SIFU ISN'T BACK WITH THE SHELVES.
I THINK WE'LL HAVE ENOUGH HELP, EVEN WITHOUT TOM AND AMY. YOU GO AHEAD.
GOOD LUCK!

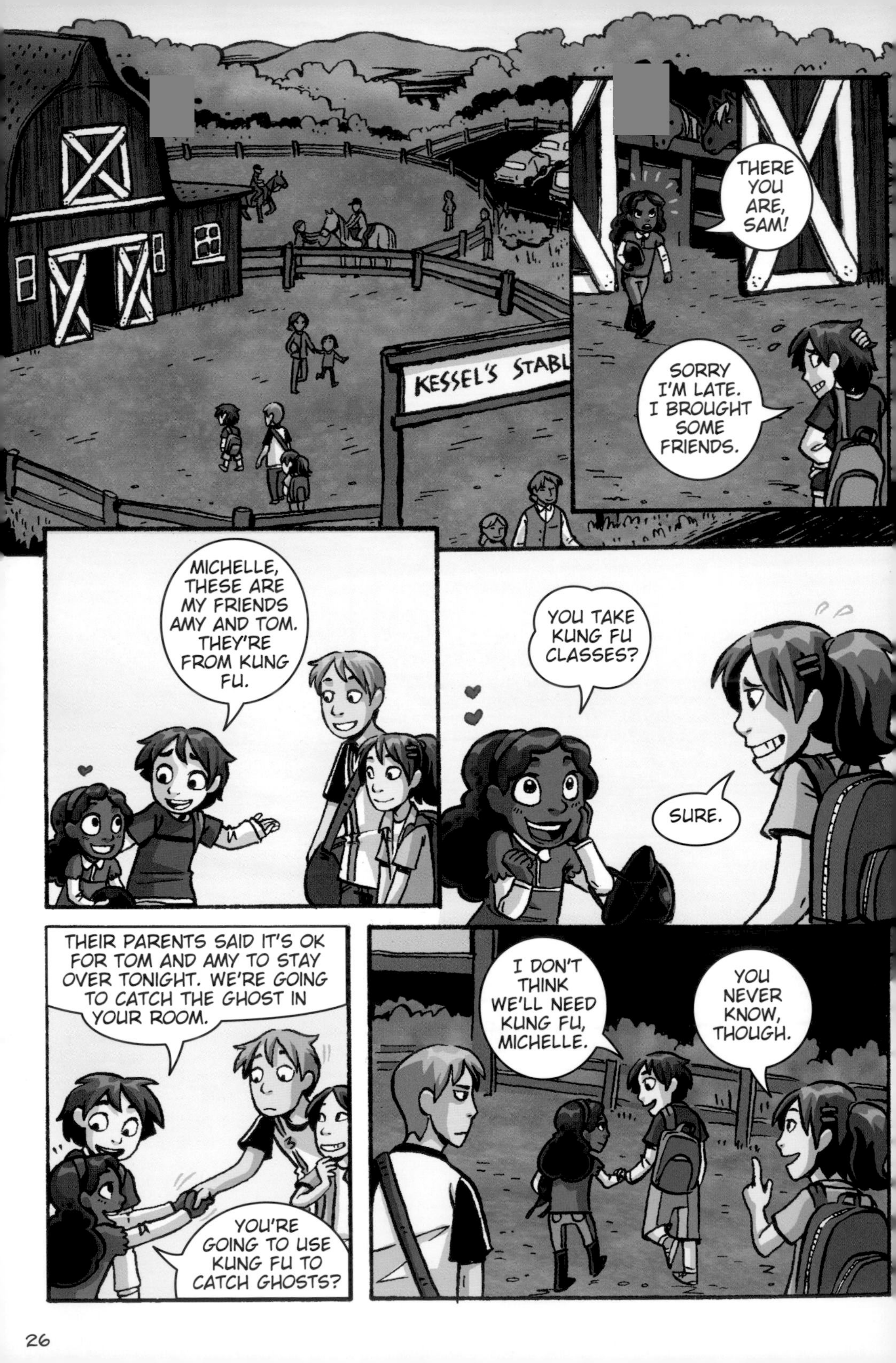
KESSEL'S STABL
THERE YOU ARE, SAM!
SORRY I'M LATE. I BROUGHT SOME FRIENDS.
MICHELLE, THESE ARE MY FRIENDS AMY AND TOM. THEY'RE FROM KUNG FU.
YOU TAKE KUNG FU CLASSES?
SURE.
THEIR PARENTS SAID IT'S OK FOR TOM AND AMY TO STAY OVER TONIGHT. WE'RE GOING TO CATCH THE GHOST IN YOUR ROOM.
YOU'RE GOING TO USE KUNG FU TO CATCH GHOSTS?
I DON'T THINK WE'LL NEED KUNG FU, MICHELLE.
YOU NEVER KNOW, THOUGH.

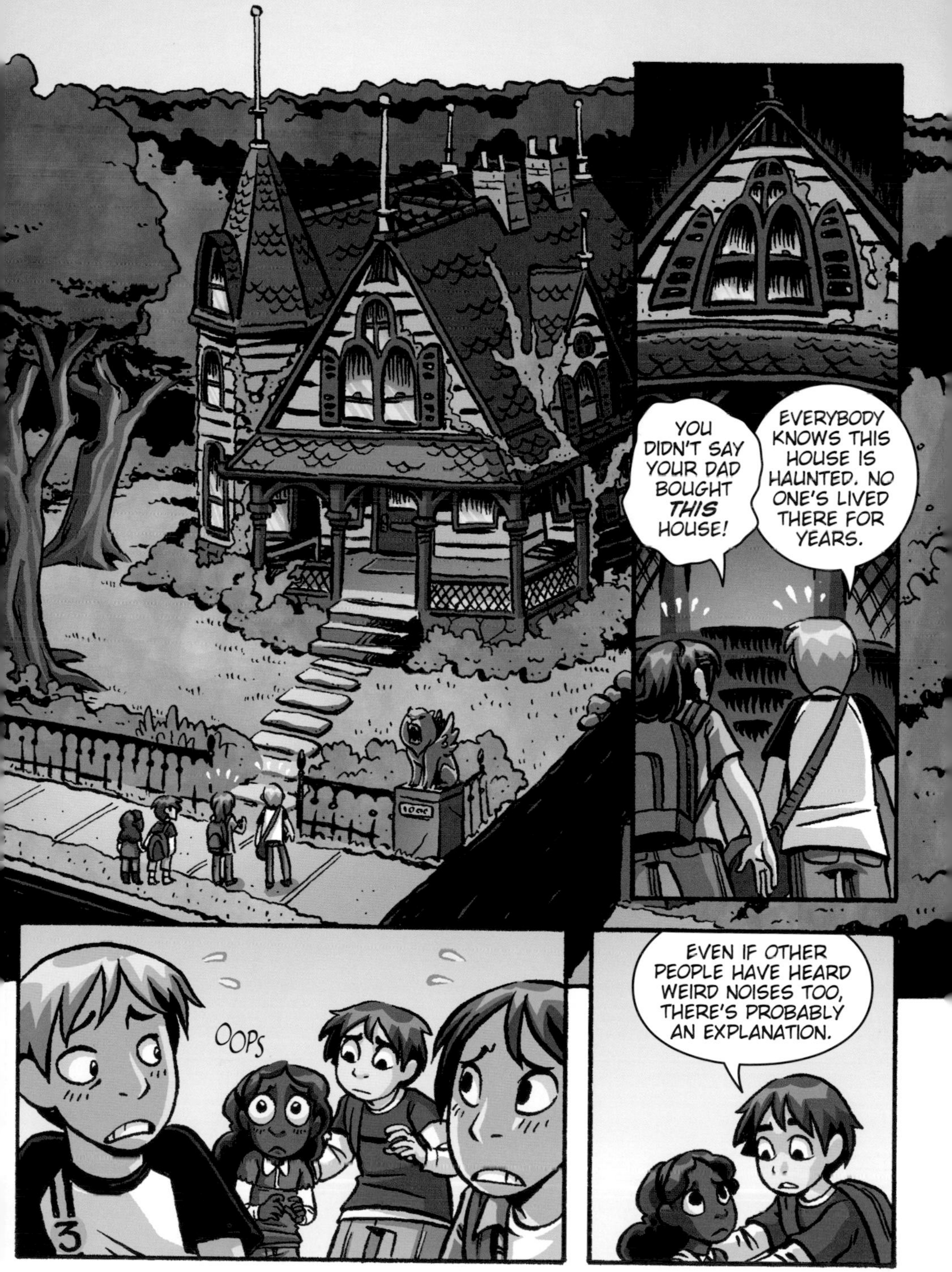

YOU DIDN'T SAY YOUR DAD BOUGHT *THIS* HOUSE!
EVERYBODY KNOWS THIS HOUSE IS HAUNTED. NO ONE'S LIVED THERE FOR YEARS.
OOPS
EVEN IF OTHER PEOPLE HAVE HEARD WEIRD NOISES TOO, THERE'S PROBABLY AN EXPLANATION.

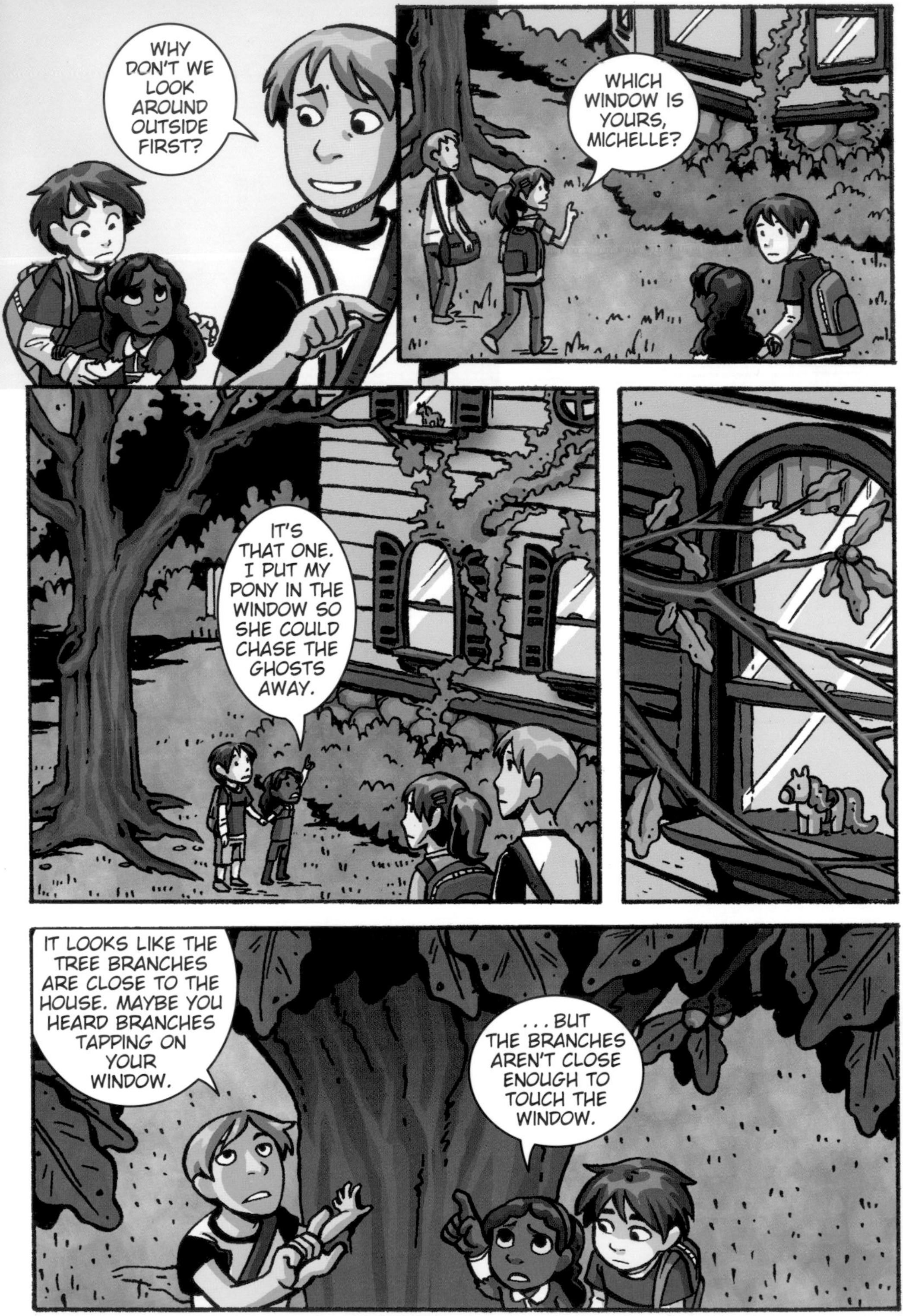
WHY DON'T WE LOOK AROUND OUTSIDE FIRST?
WHICH WINDOW IS YOURS, MICHELLE?
IT'S THAT ONE. I PUT MY PONY IN THE WINDOW SO SHE COULD CHASE THE GHOSTS AWAY.
IT LOOKS LIKE THE TREE BRANCHES ARE CLOSE TO THE HOUSE. MAYBE YOU HEARD BRANCHES TAPPING ON YOUR WINDOW.
. . . BUT THE BRANCHES AREN'T CLOSE ENOUGH TO TOUCH THE WINDOW.

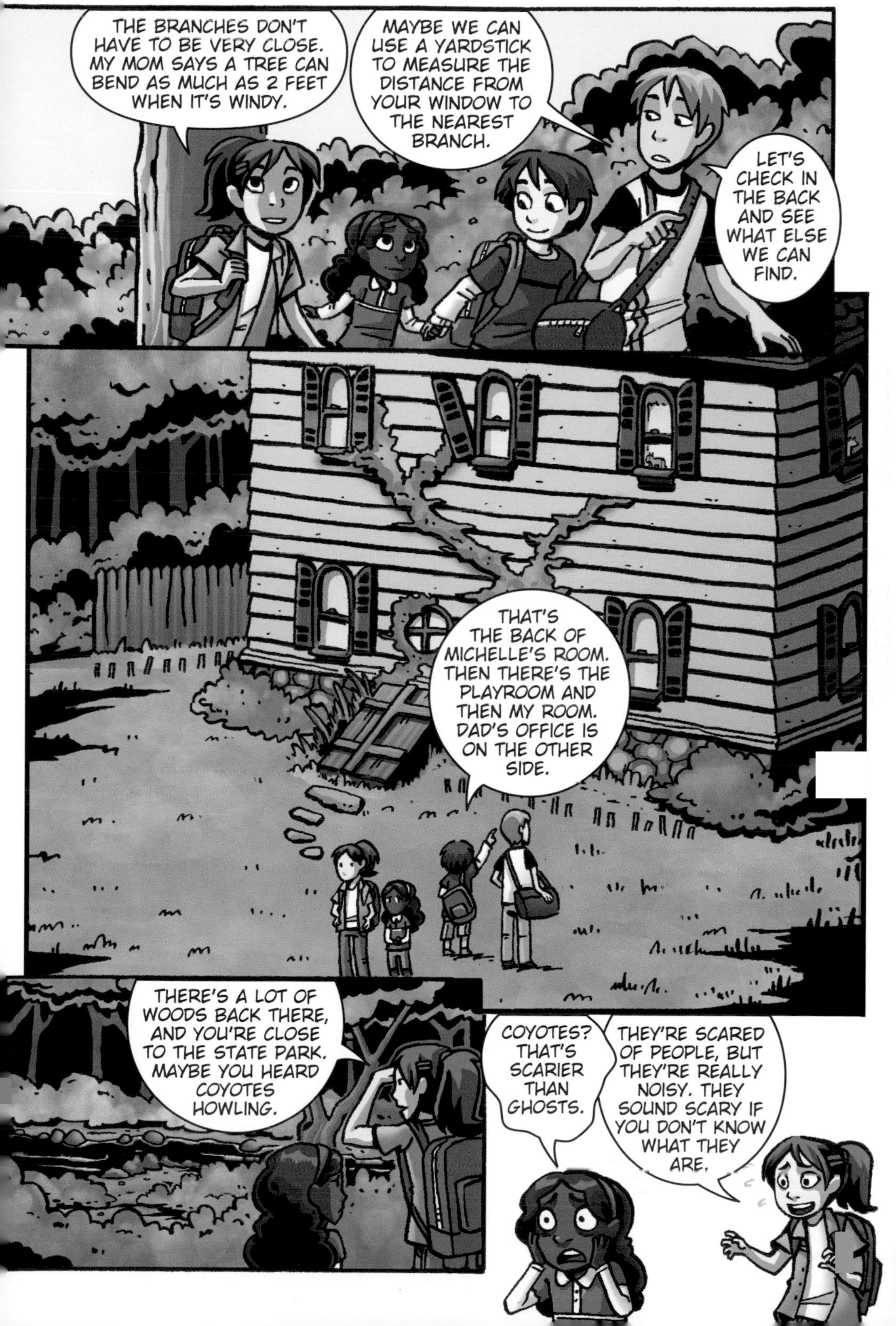
THE BRANCHES DON'T HAVE TO BE VERY CLOSE. MY MOM SAYS A TREE CAN BEND AS MUCH AS 2 FEET WHEN IT'S WINDY.
MAYBE WE CAN USE A YARDSTICK TO MEASURE THE DISTANCE FROM YOUR WINDOW TO THE NEAREST BRANCH.
LET'S CHECK IN THE BACK AND SEE WHAT ELSE WE CAN FIND.
THAT'S THE BACK OF MICHELLE'S ROOM. THEN THERE'S THE PLAYROOM AND THEN MY ROOM. DAD'S OFFICE IS ON THE OTHER SIDE.
THERE'S A LOT OF WOODS BACK THERE, AND YOU'RE CLOSE TO THE STATE PARK. MAYBE YOU HEARD COYOTES HOWLING.
COYOTES? THAT'S SCARIER THAN GHOSTS.
THEY'RE SCARED OF PEOPLE, BUT THEY'RE REALLY NOISY. THEY SOUND SCARY IF YOU DON'T KNOW WHAT THEY ARE.

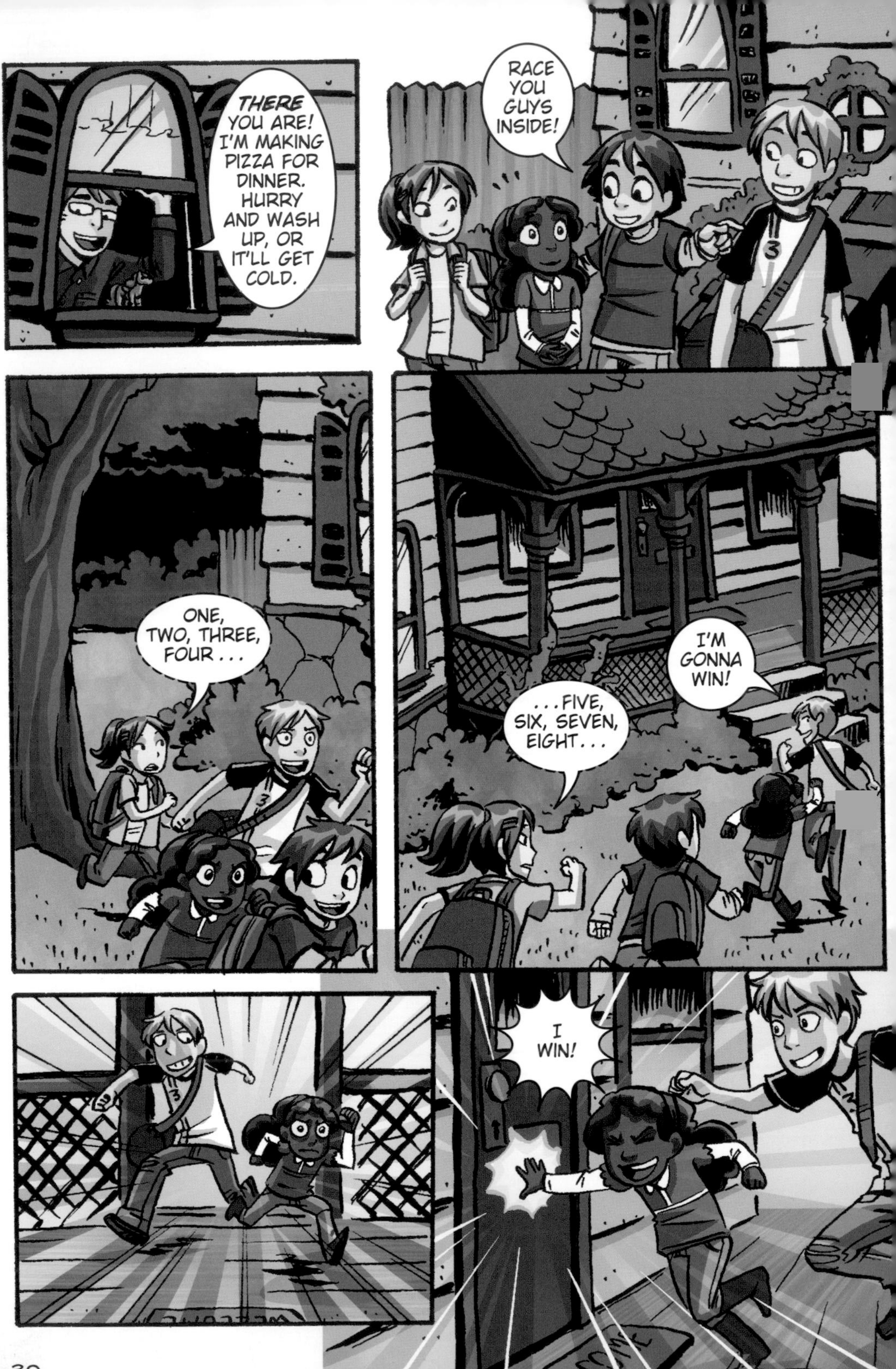
THERE YOU ARE! I'M MAKING PIZZA FOR DINNER. HURRY AND WASH UP, OR IT'LL GET COLD.
RACE YOU GUYS INSIDE!
ONE, TWO, THREE, FOUR . . .
. . .FIVE, SIX, SEVEN, EIGHT . . .
I'M GONNA WIN!
I WIN!

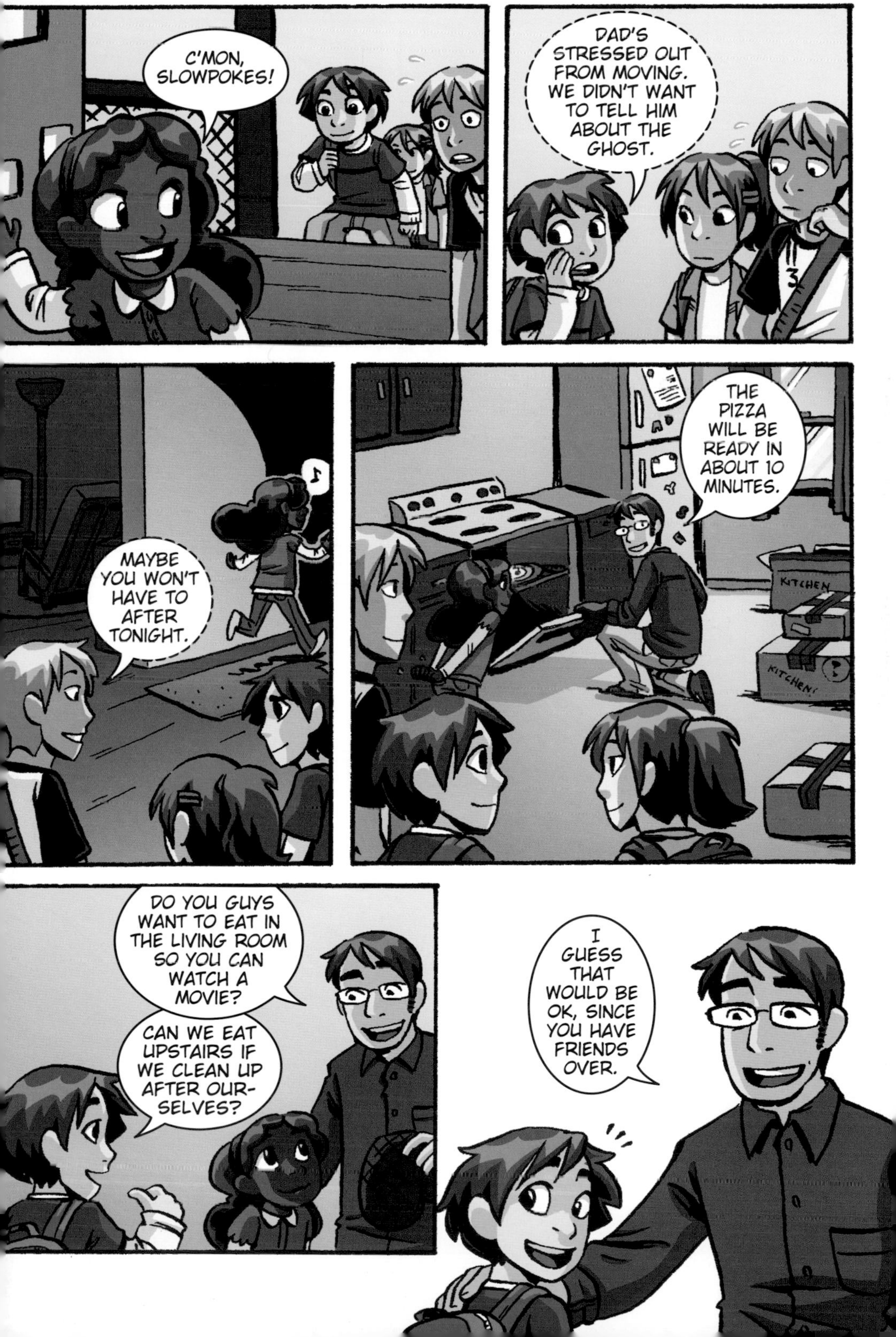

C'MON, SLOWPOKES!
DAD'S STRESSED OUT FROM MOVING. WE DIDN'T WANT TO TELL HIM ABOUT THE GHOST.
MAYBE YOU WON'T HAVE TO AFTER TONIGHT.
THE PIZZA WILL BE READY IN ABOUT 10 MINUTES.
KITCHEN
KITCHEN
DO YOU GUYS WANT TO EAT IN THE LIVING ROOM SO YOU CAN WATCH A MOVIE?
CAN WE EAT UPSTAIRS IF WE CLEAN UP AFTER OUR-SELVES?
I GUESS THAT WOULD BE OK, SINCE YOU HAVE FRIENDS OVER.

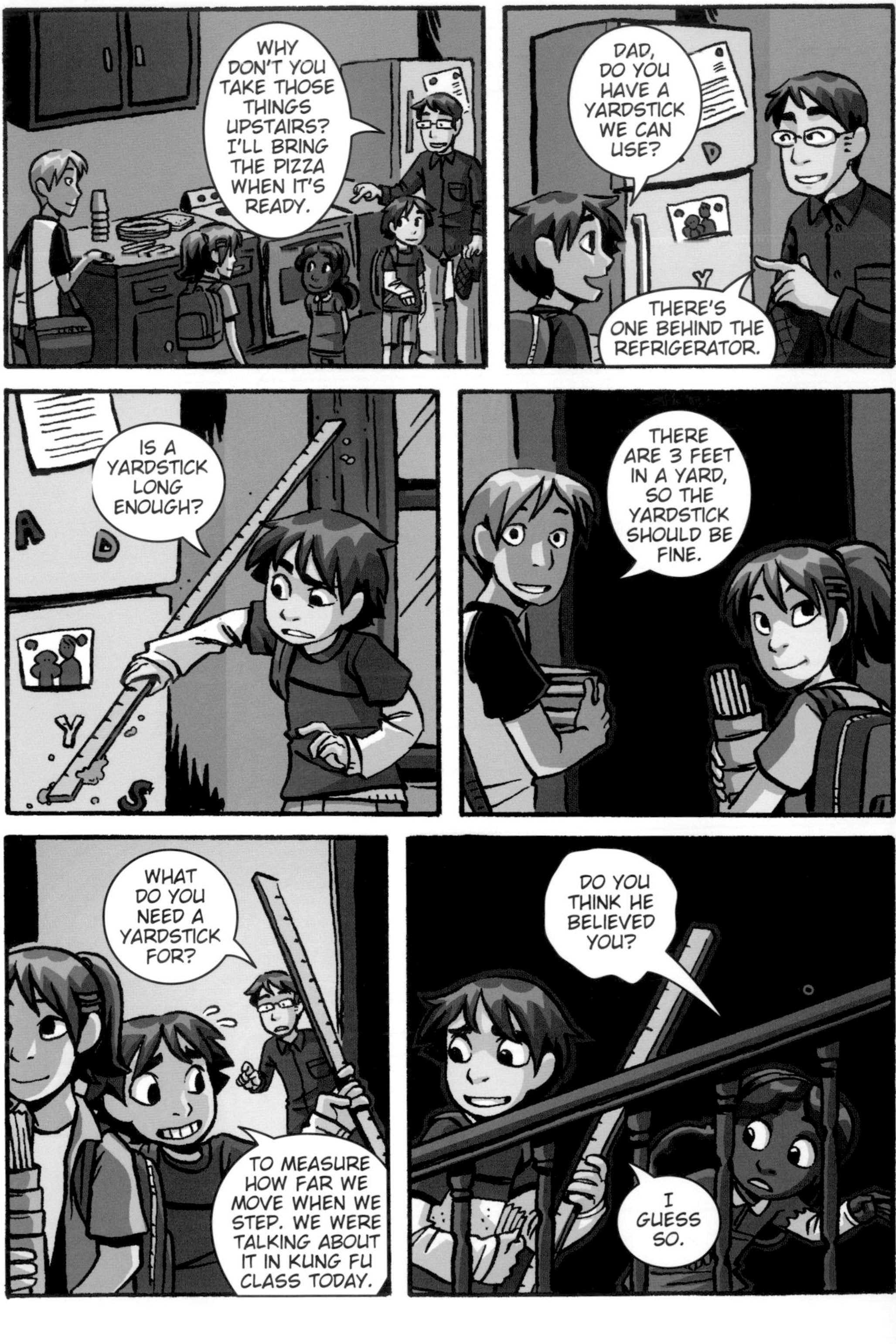
WHY DON'T YOU TAKE THOSE THINGS UPSTAIRS? I'LL BRING THE PIZZA WHEN IT'S READY.
DAD, DO YOU HAVE A YARDSTICK WE CAN USE?
THERE'S ONE BEHIND THE REFRIGERATOR.
IS A YARDSTICK LONG ENOUGH?
THERE ARE 3 FEET IN A YARD, SO THE YARDSTICK SHOULD BE FINE.
WHAT DO YOU NEED A YARDSTICK FOR?
TO MEASURE HOW FAR WE MOVE WHEN WE STEP. WE WERE TALKING ABOUT IT IN KUNG FU CLASS TODAY.
DO YOU THINK HE BELIEVED YOU?
I GUESS SO.

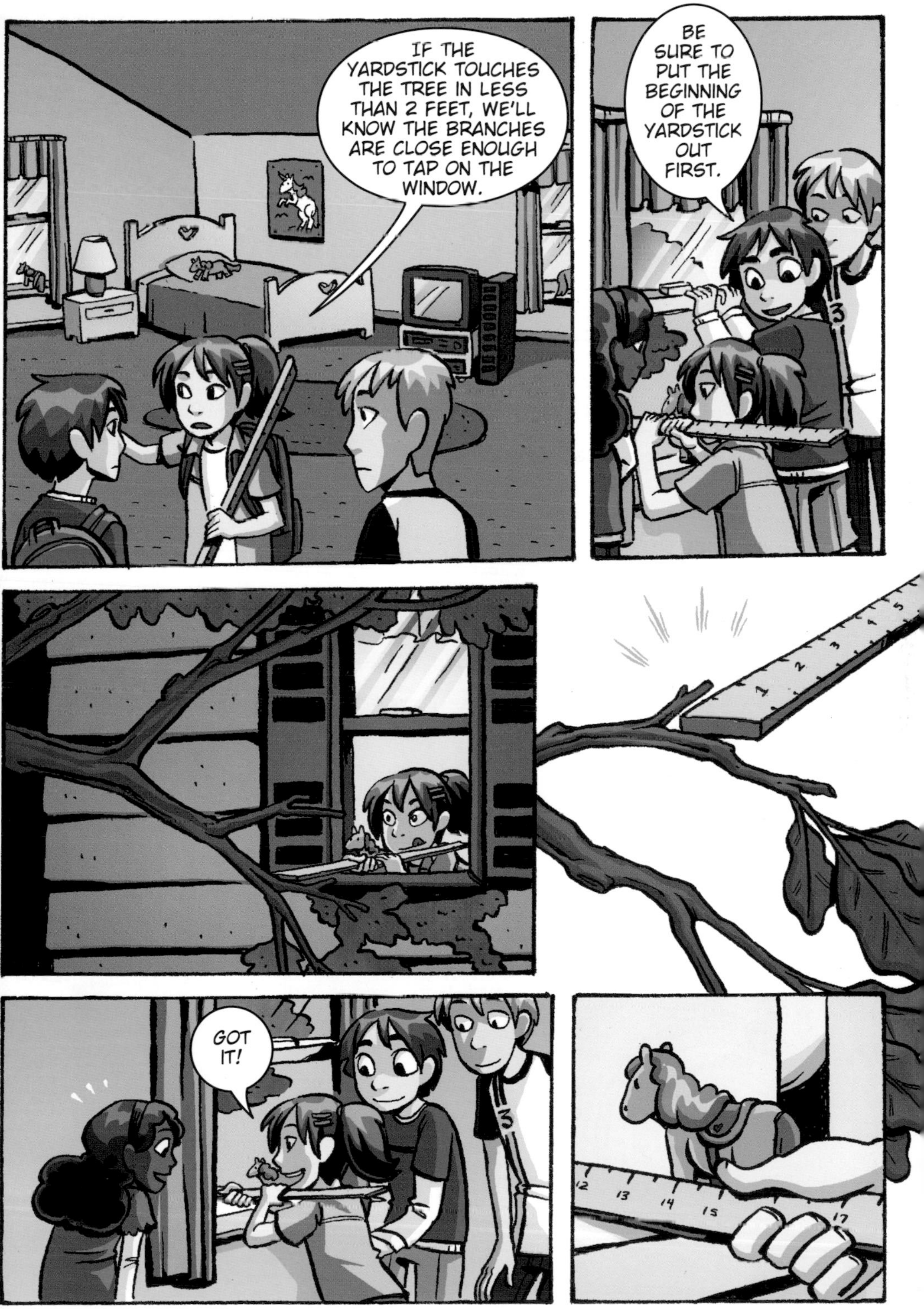
IF THE YARDSTICK TOUCHES THE TREE IN LESS THAN 2 FEET, WE'LL KNOW THE BRANCHES ARE CLOSE ENOUGH TO TAP ON THE WINDOW.
BE SURE TO PUT THE BEGINNING OF THE YARDSTICK OUT FIRST.
GOT IT!

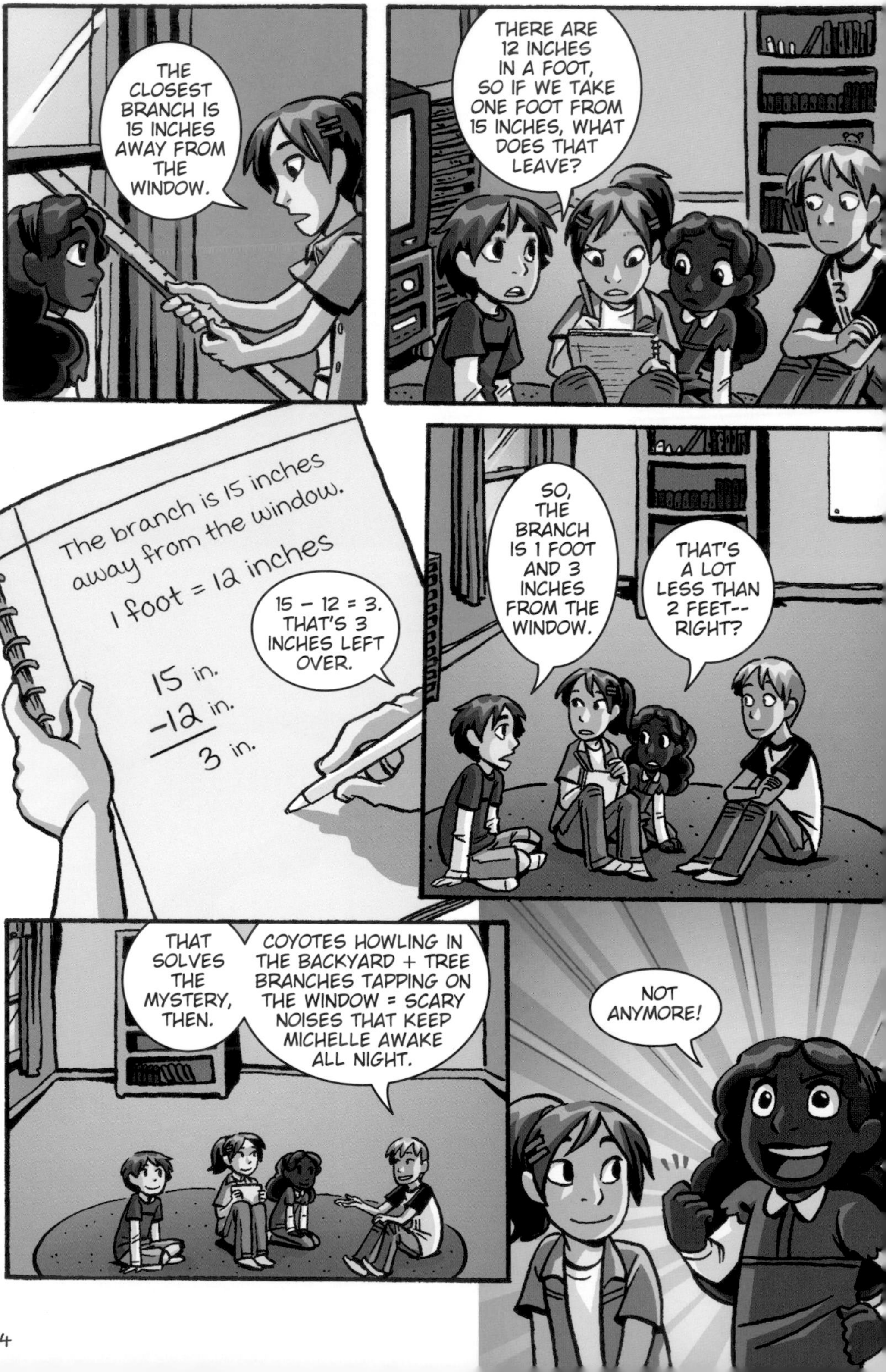
THE CLOSEST BRANCH IS 15 INCHES AWAY FROM THE WINDOW.
THERE ARE 12 INCHES IN A FOOT, SO IF WE TAKE ONE FOOT FROM 15 INCHES, WHAT DOES THAT LEAVE?
The branch is 15 inches away from the window.
1 foot = 12 inches
15 in.
-12 in.
3 in.
15 – 12 = 3. THAT'S 3 INCHES LEFT OVER.
SO, THE BRANCH IS 1 FOOT AND 3 INCHES FROM THE WINDOW.
THAT'S A LOT LESS THAN 2 FEET--RIGHT?
THAT SOLVES THE MYSTERY, THEN.
COYOTES HOWLING IN THE BACKYARD + TREE BRANCHES TAPPING ON THE WINDOW = SCARY NOISES THAT KEEP MICHELLE AWAKE ALL NIGHT.
NOT ANYMORE!

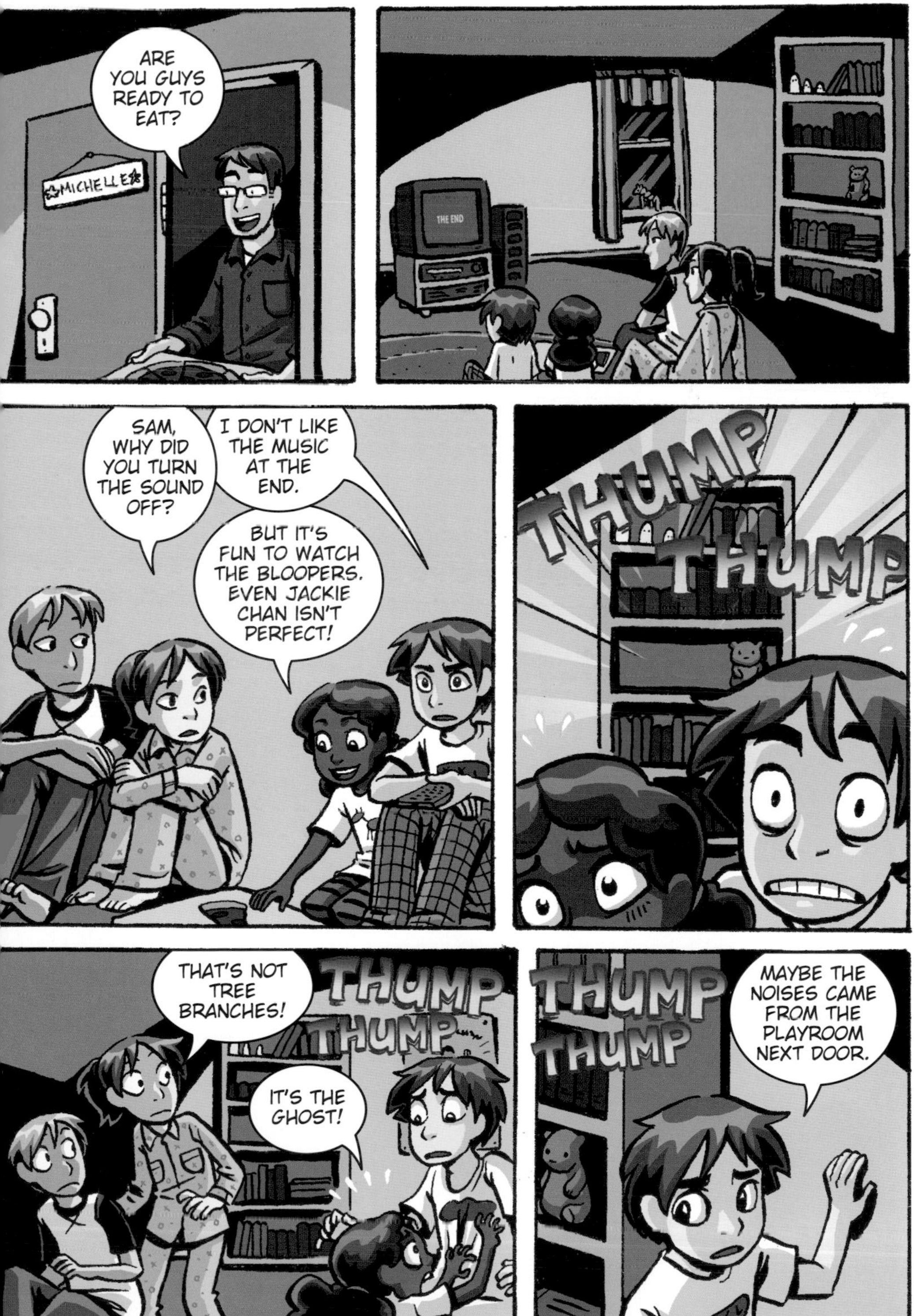
ARE YOU GUYS READY TO EAT?
MICHELLE
THE END
SAM, WHY DID YOU TURN THE SOUND OFF?
I DON'T LIKE THE MUSIC AT THE END.
BUT IT'S FUN TO WATCH THE BLOOPERS. EVEN JACKIE CHAN ISN'T PERFECT!
THUMP
THUMP
THAT'S NOT TREE BRANCHES!
THUMP
THUMP
IT'S THE GHOST!
THUMP
THUMP
MAYBE THE NOISES CAME FROM THE PLAYROOM NEXT DOOR.

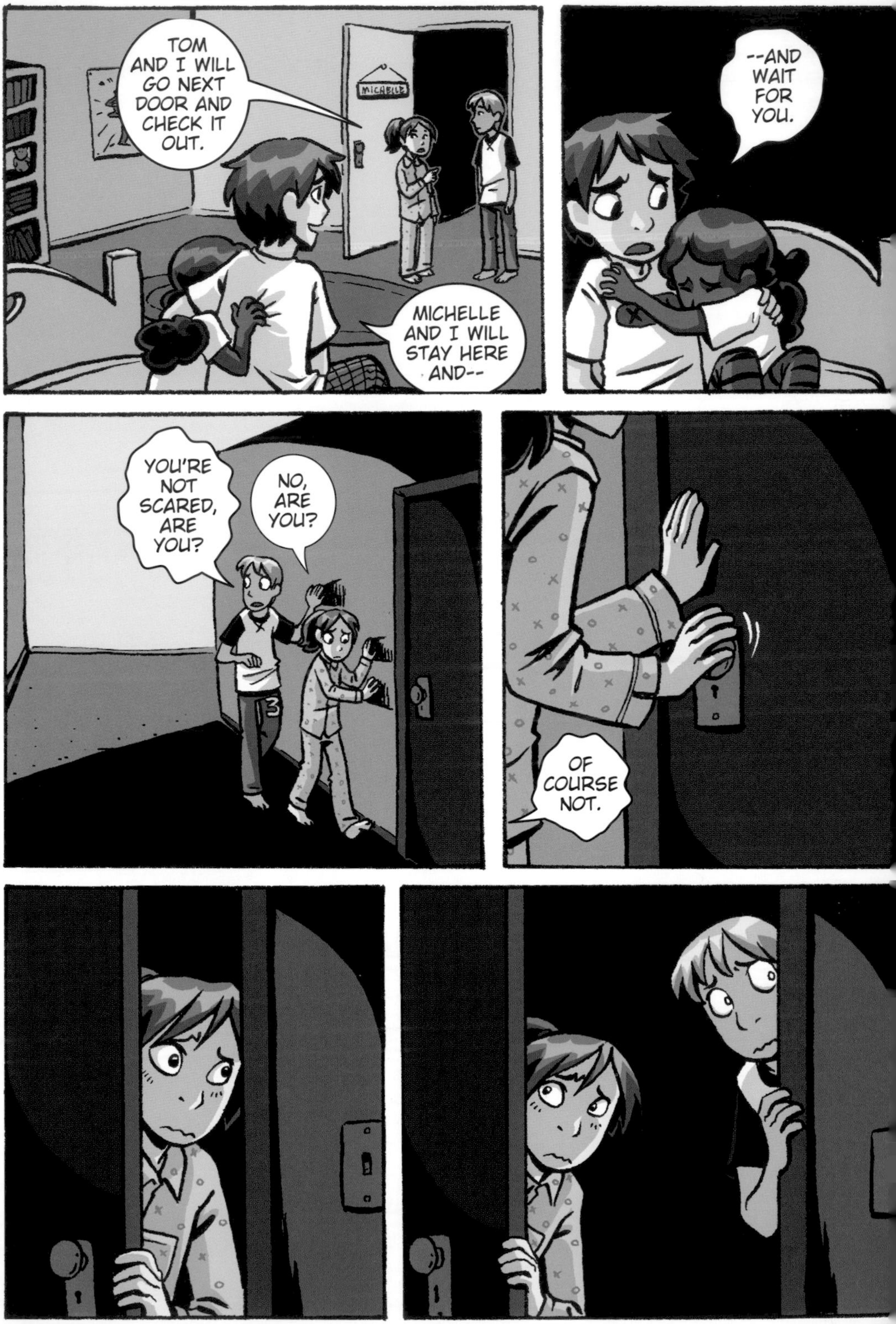
TOM AND I WILL GO NEXT DOOR AND CHECK IT OUT.
MICHELLE AND I WILL STAY HERE AND--
--AND WAIT FOR YOU.
YOU'RE NOT SCARED, ARE YOU?
NO, ARE YOU?
OF COURSE NOT.

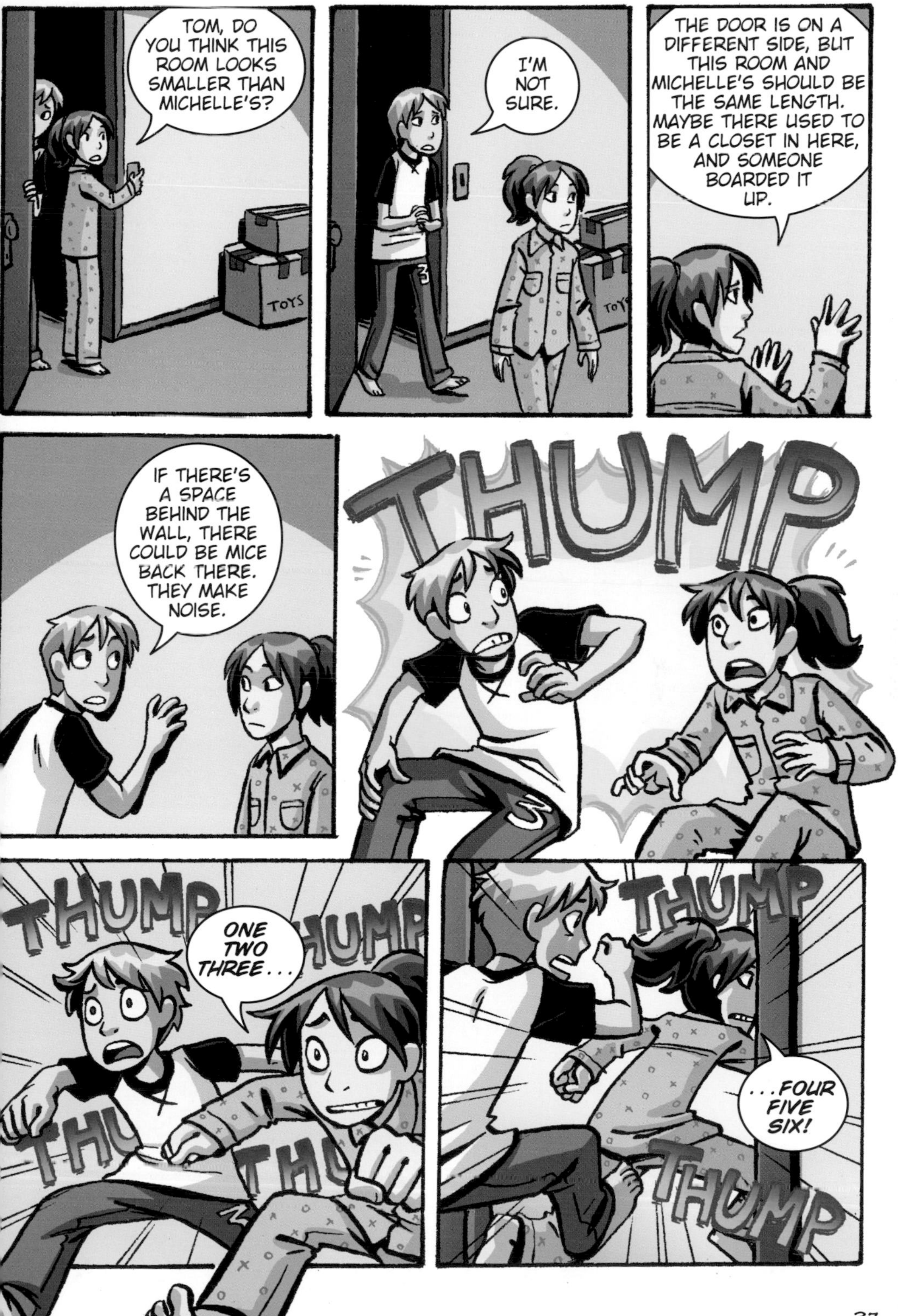
TOM, DO YOU THINK THIS ROOM LOOKS SMALLER THAN MICHELLE'S?
TOYS
I'M NOT SURE.
TOYS
THE DOOR IS ON A DIFFERENT SIDE, BUT THIS ROOM AND MICHELLE'S SHOULD BE THE SAME LENGTH. MAYBE THERE USED TO BE A CLOSET IN HERE, AND SOMEONE BOARDED IT UP.
IF THERE'S A SPACE BEHIND THE WALL, THERE COULD BE MICE BACK THERE. THEY MAKE NOISE.
THUMP
THUMP
THUMP
ONE TWO THREE. . .
THUMP
...FOUR FIVE SIX!
THUMP

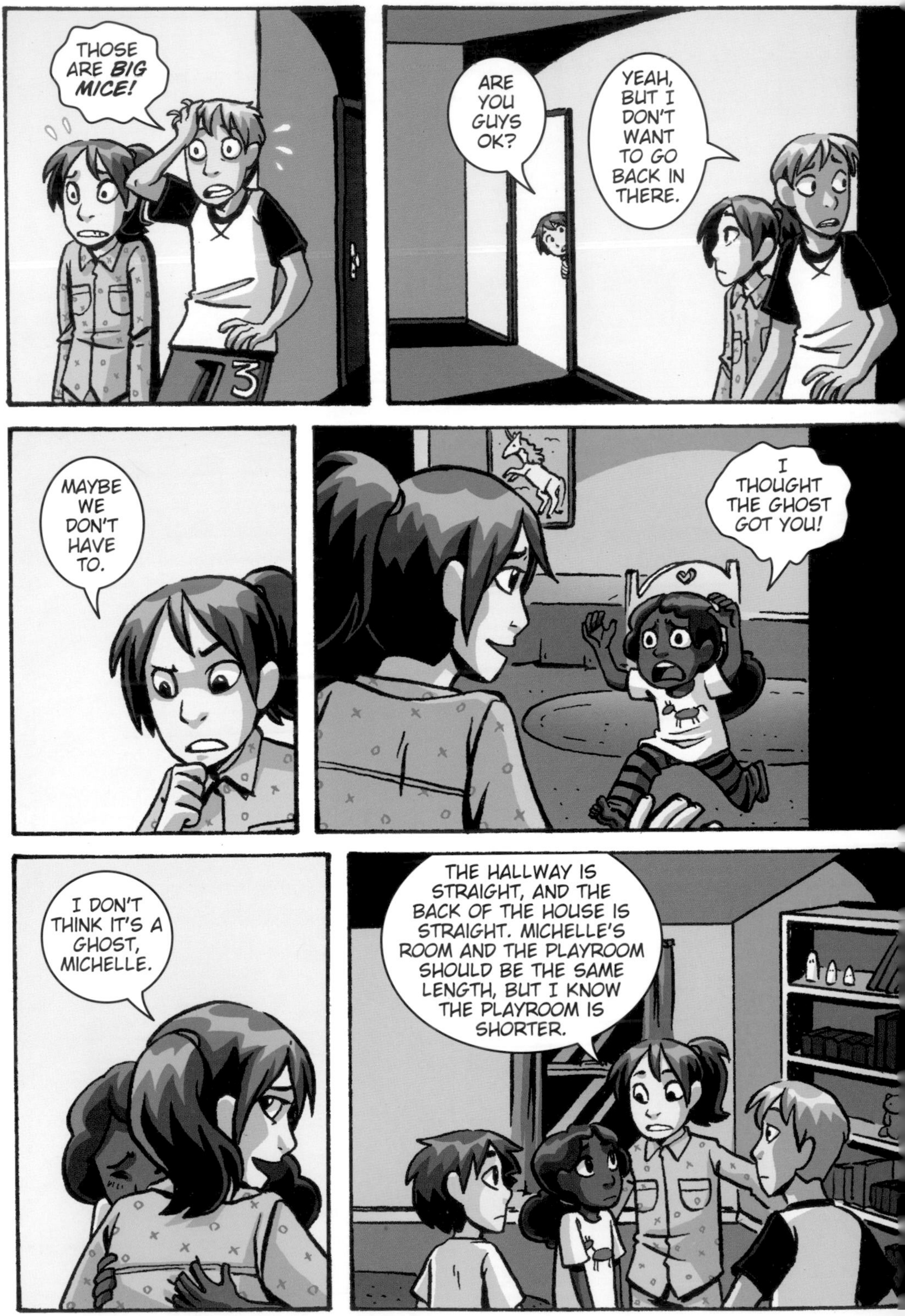
THOSE ARE BIG MICE!
ARE YOU GUYS OK?
YEAH, BUT I DON'T WANT TO GO BACK IN THERE.
MAYBE WE DON'T HAVE TO.
I THOUGHT THE GHOST GOT YOU!
I DON'T THINK IT'S A GHOST, MICHELLE.
THE HALLWAY IS STRAIGHT, AND THE BACK OF THE HOUSE IS STRAIGHT. MICHELLE'S ROOM AND THE PLAYROOM SHOULD BE THE SAME LENGTH, BUT I KNOW THE PLAYROOM IS SHORTER.

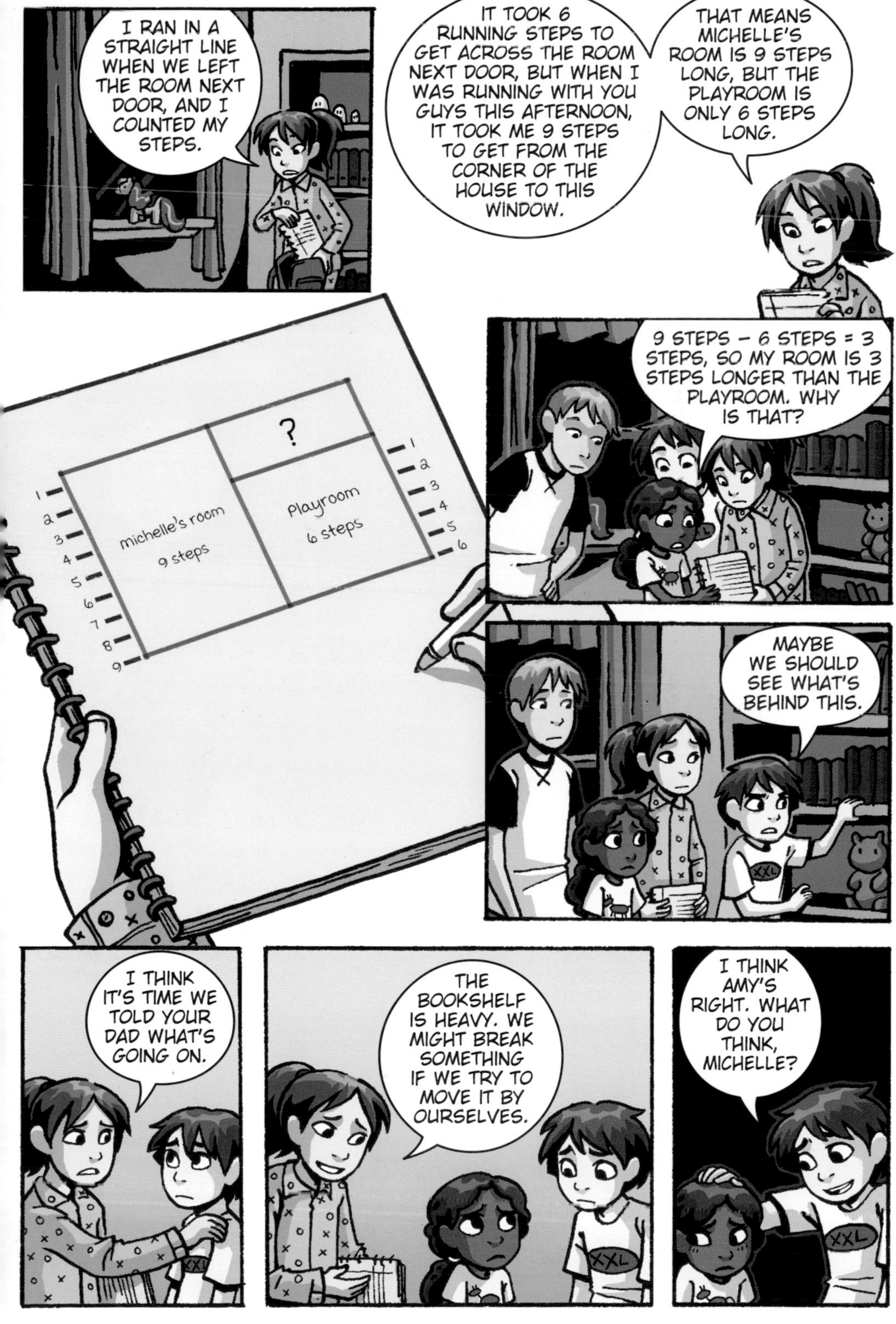
I RAN IN A STRAIGHT LINE WHEN WE LEFT THE ROOM NEXT DOOR, AND I COUNTED MY STEPS.
IT TOOK 6 RUNNING STEPS TO GET ACROSS THE ROOM NEXT DOOR, BUT WHEN I WAS RUNNING WITH YOU GUYS THIS AFTERNOON, IT TOOK ME 9 STEPS TO GET FROM THE CORNER OF THE HOUSE TO THIS WINDOW.
THAT MEANS MICHELLE'S ROOM IS 9 STEPS LONG, BUT THE PLAYROOM IS ONLY 6 STEPS LONG.
?
michelle's room
9 steps
Playroom
6 steps
1
2
3
4
5
6
7
8
9
1
2
3
4
5
6
9 STEPS – 6 STEPS = 3 STEPS, SO MY ROOM IS 3 STEPS LONGER THAN THE PLAYROOM. WHY IS THAT?
MAYBE WE SHOULD SEE WHAT'S BEHIND THIS.
XXL
I THINK IT'S TIME WE TOLD YOUR DAD WHAT'S GOING ON.
THE BOOKSHELF IS HEAVY. WE MIGHT BREAK SOMETHING IF WE TRY TO MOVE IT BY OURSELVES.
I THINK AMY'S RIGHT. WHAT DO YOU THINK, MICHELLE?

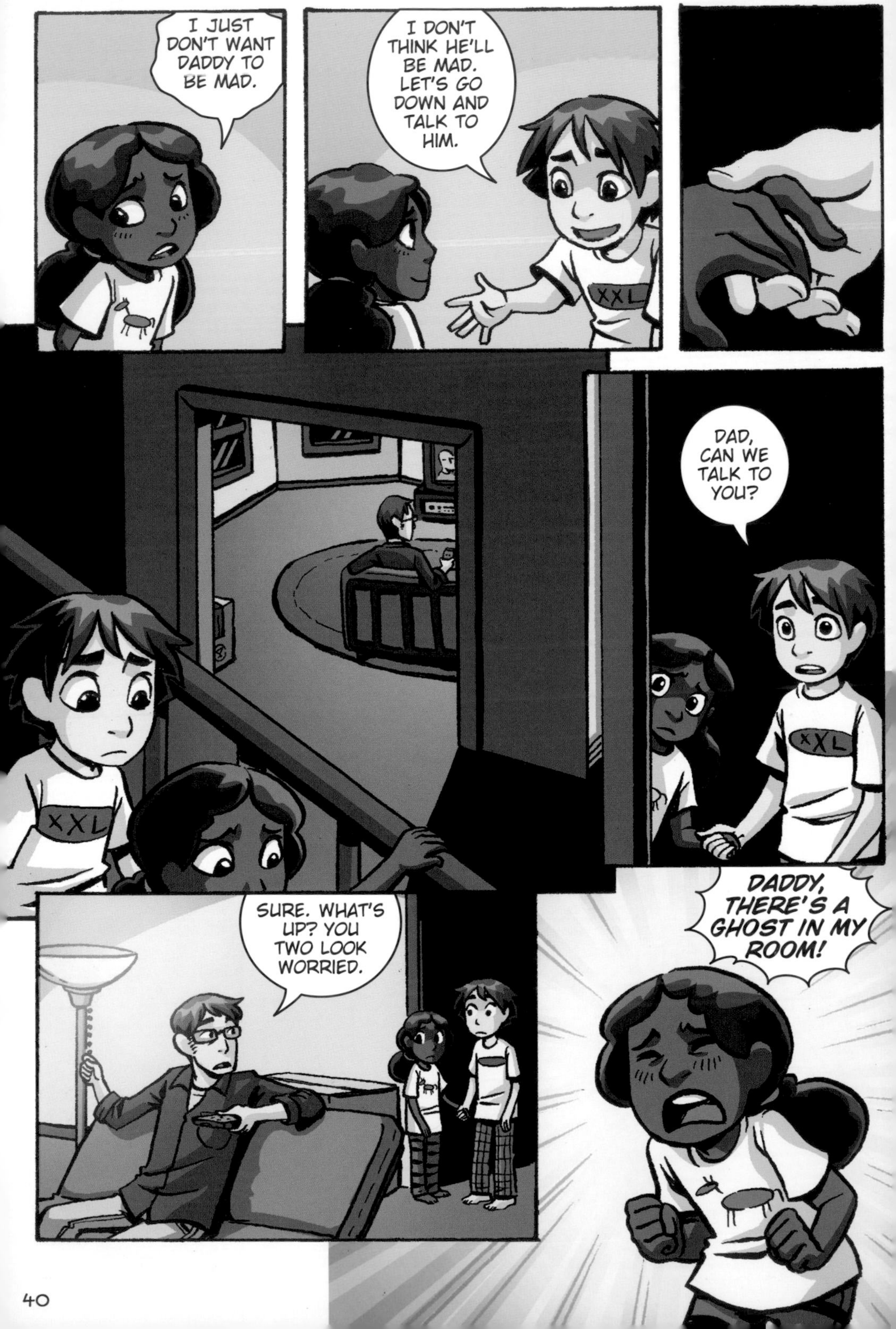

I JUST DON'T WANT DADDY TO BE MAD.
I DON'T THINK HE'LL BE MAD. LET'S GO DOWN AND TALK TO HIM.
XXL
XXL
DAD, CAN WE TALK TO YOU?
XXL
SURE. WHAT'S UP? YOU TWO LOOK WORRIED.
DADDY, THERE'S A GHOST IN MY ROOM!

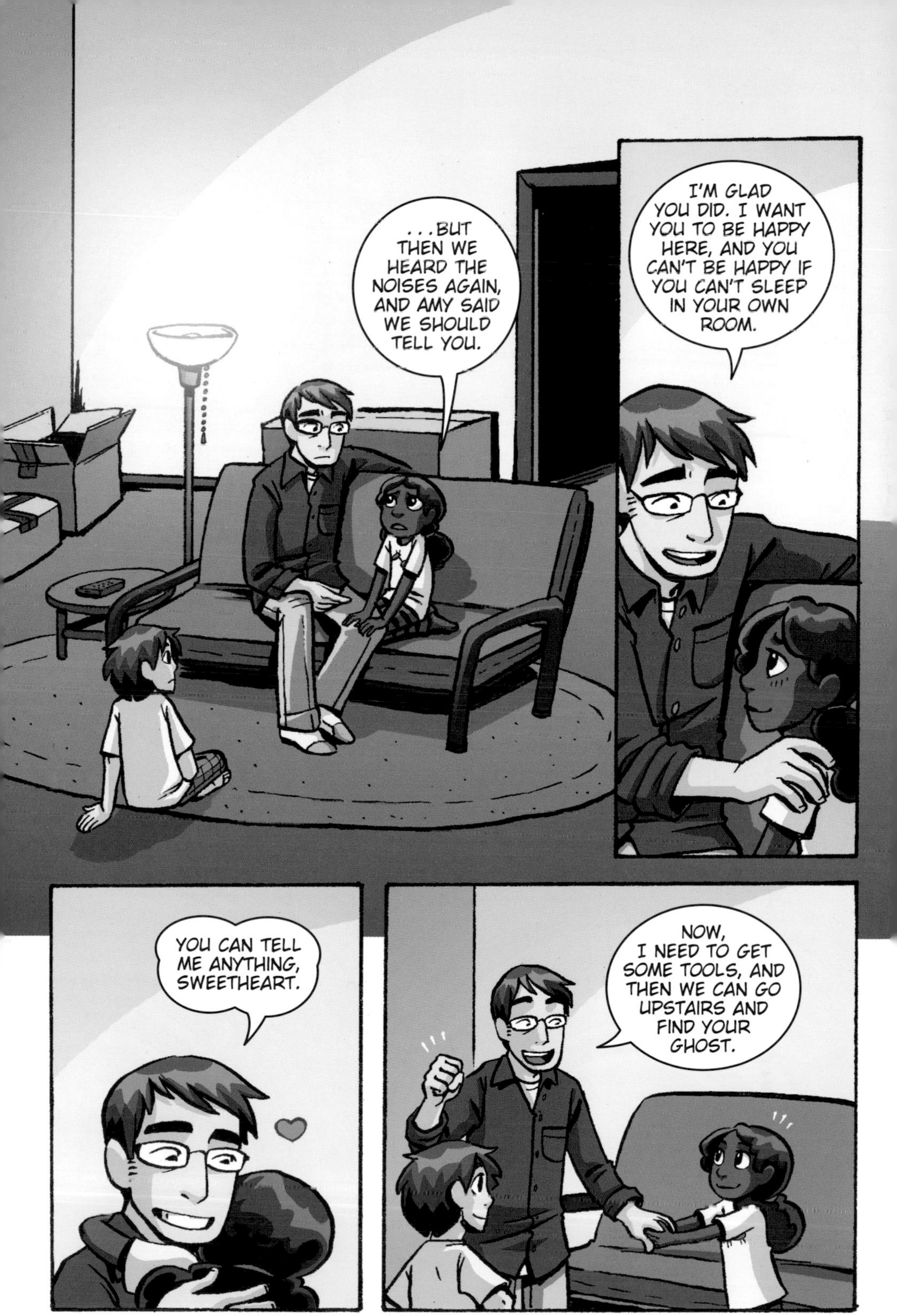

...BUT THEN WE HEARD THE NOISES AGAIN, AND AMY SAID WE SHOULD TELL YOU.
I'M GLAD YOU DID. I WANT YOU TO BE HAPPY HERE, AND YOU CAN'T BE HAPPY IF YOU CAN'T SLEEP IN YOUR OWN ROOM.
YOU CAN TELL ME ANYTHING, SWEETHEART.
NOW, I NEED TO GET SOME TOOLS, AND THEN WE CAN GO UPSTAIRS AND FIND YOUR GHOST.

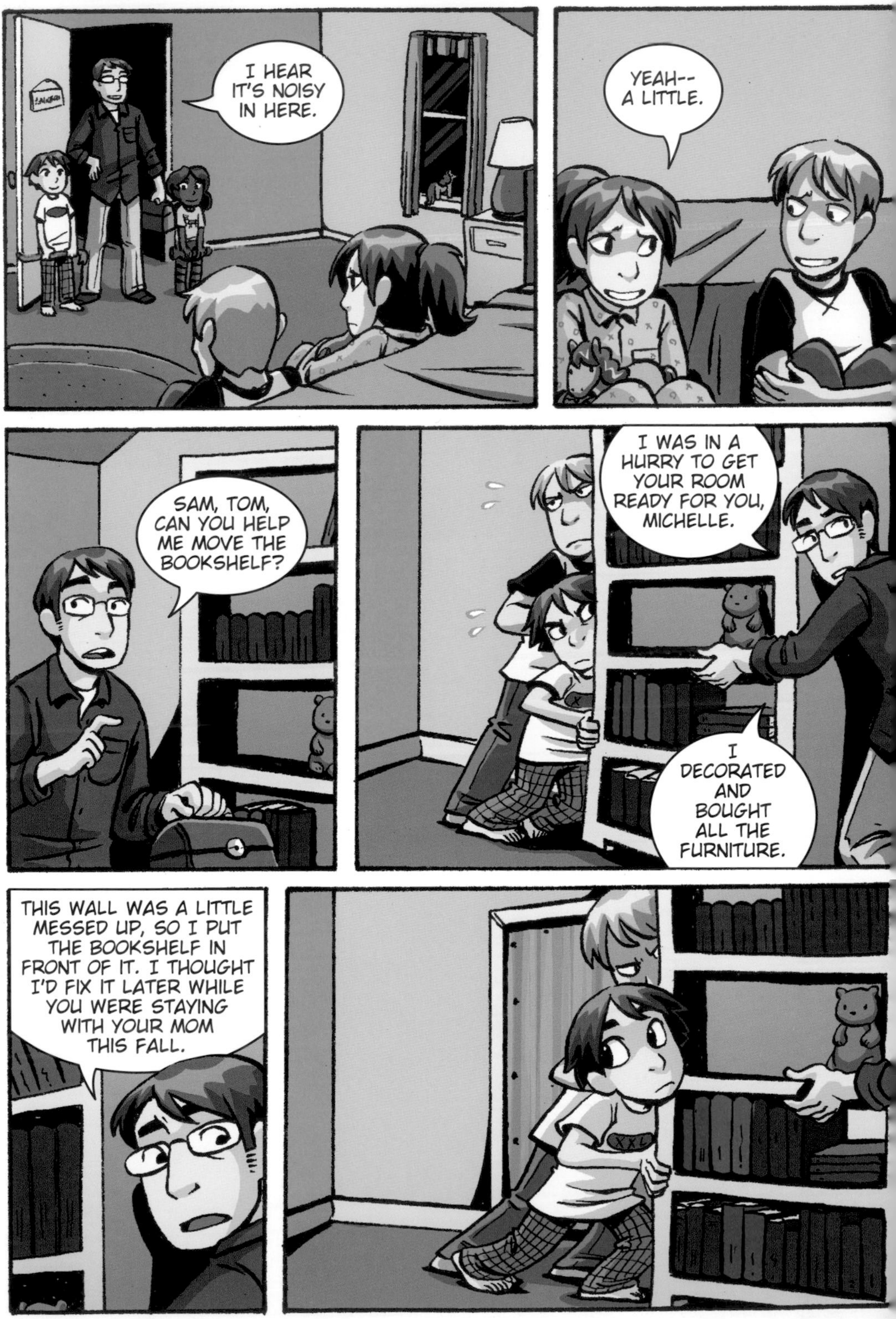
I HEAR IT'S NOISY IN HERE.
YEAH-- A LITTLE.
SAM, TOM, CAN YOU HELP ME MOVE THE BOOKSHELF?
I WAS IN A HURRY TO GET YOUR ROOM READY FOR YOU, MICHELLE.
I DECORATED AND BOUGHT ALL THE FURNITURE.
THIS WALL WAS A LITTLE MESSED UP, SO I PUT THE BOOKSHELF IN FRONT OF IT. I THOUGHT I'D FIX IT LATER WHILE YOU WERE STAYING WITH YOUR MOM THIS FALL.

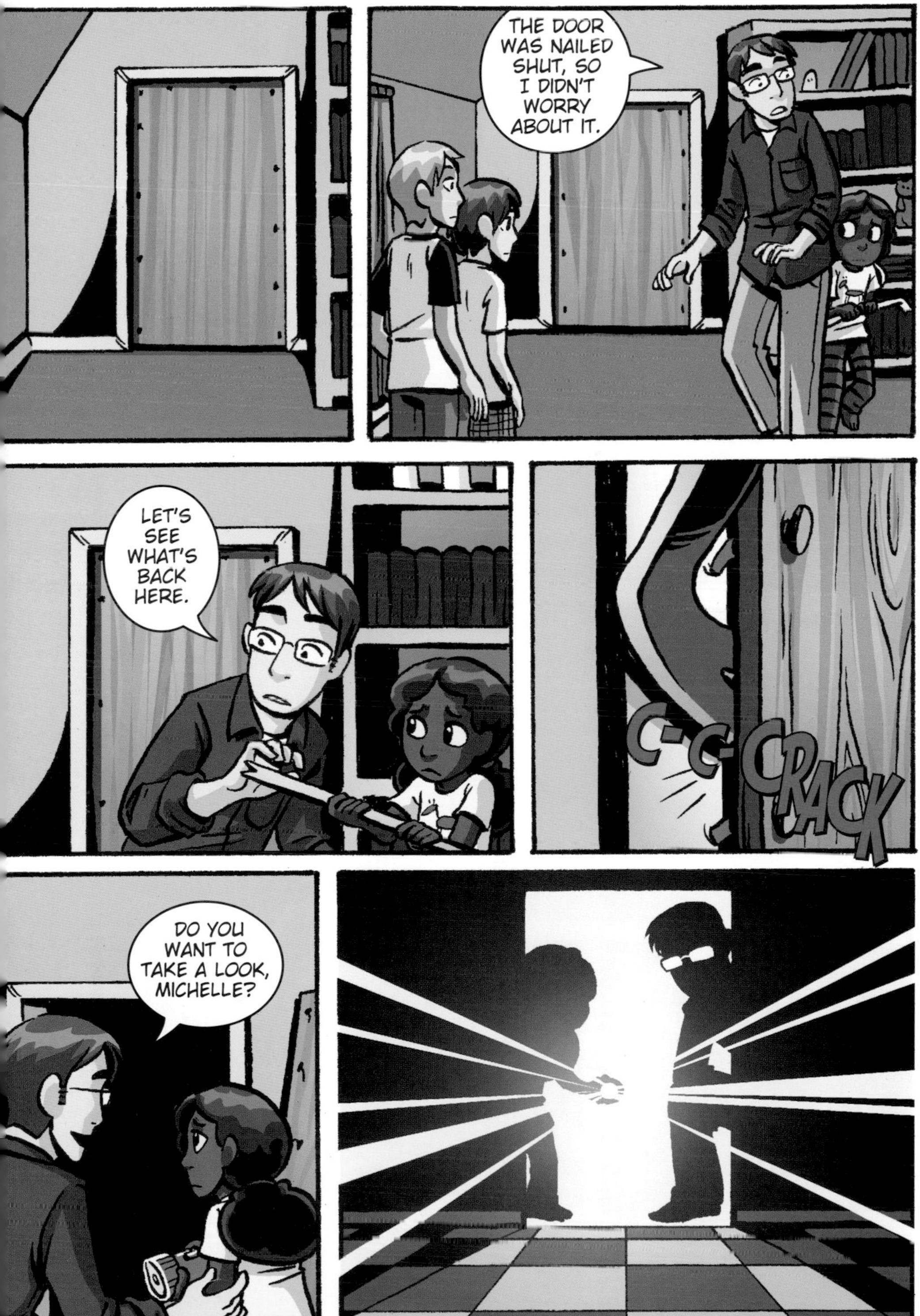
THE DOOR WAS NAILED SHUT, SO I DIDN'T WORRY ABOUT IT.
LET'S SEE WHAT'S BACK HERE.
C-C-CRACK
DO YOU WANT TO TAKE A LOOK, MICHELLE?

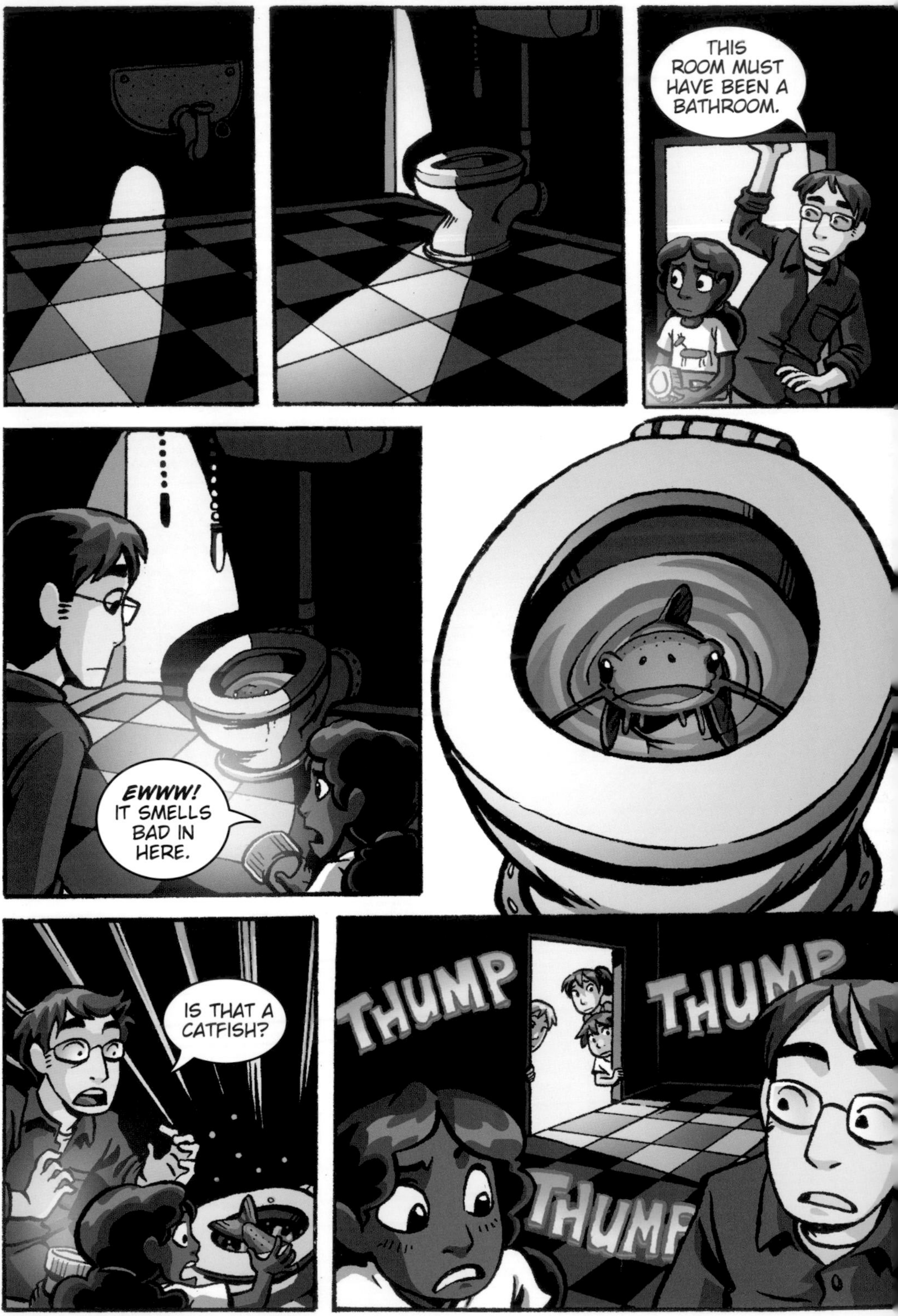
THIS ROOM MUST HAVE BEEN A BATHROOM.
EWWW! IT SMELLS BAD IN HERE.
IS THAT A CATFISH?
THUMP
THUMP
THUMP

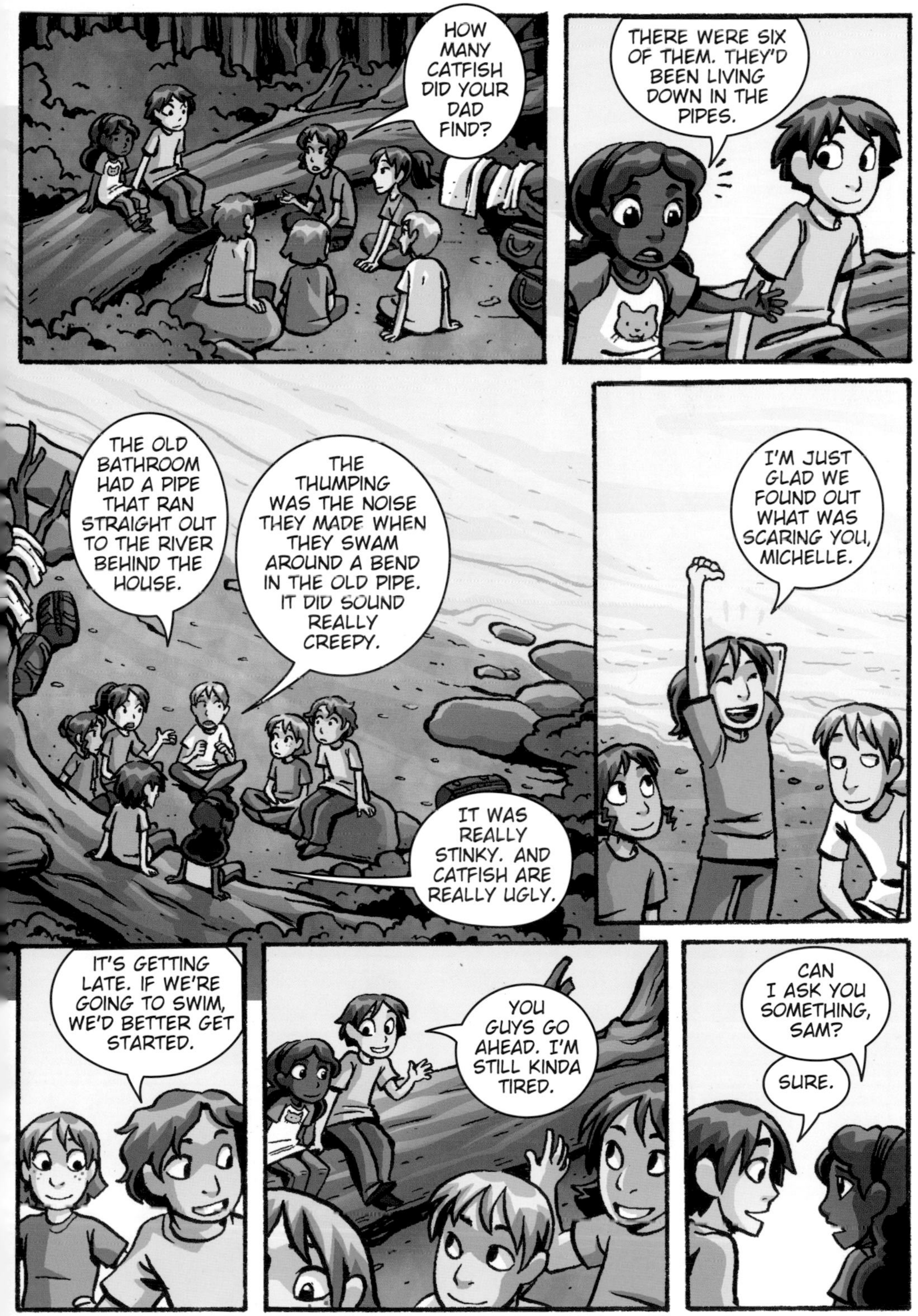
HOW MANY CATFISH DID YOUR DAD FIND?
THERE WERE SIX OF THEM. THEY'D BEEN LIVING DOWN IN THE PIPES.
THE OLD BATHROOM HAD A PIPE THAT RAN STRAIGHT OUT TO THE RIVER BEHIND THE HOUSE.
THE THUMPING WAS THE NOISE THEY MADE WHEN THEY SWAM AROUND A BEND IN THE OLD PIPE. IT DID SOUND REALLY CREEPY.
IT WAS REALLY STINKY. AND CATFISH ARE REALLY UGLY.
I'M JUST GLAD WE FOUND OUT WHAT WAS SCARING YOU, MICHELLE.
IT'S GETTING LATE. IF WE'RE GOING TO SWIM, WE'D BETTER GET STARTED.
YOU GUYS GO AHEAD. I'M STILL KINDA TIRED.
CAN I ASK YOU SOMETHING, SAM?
SURE.

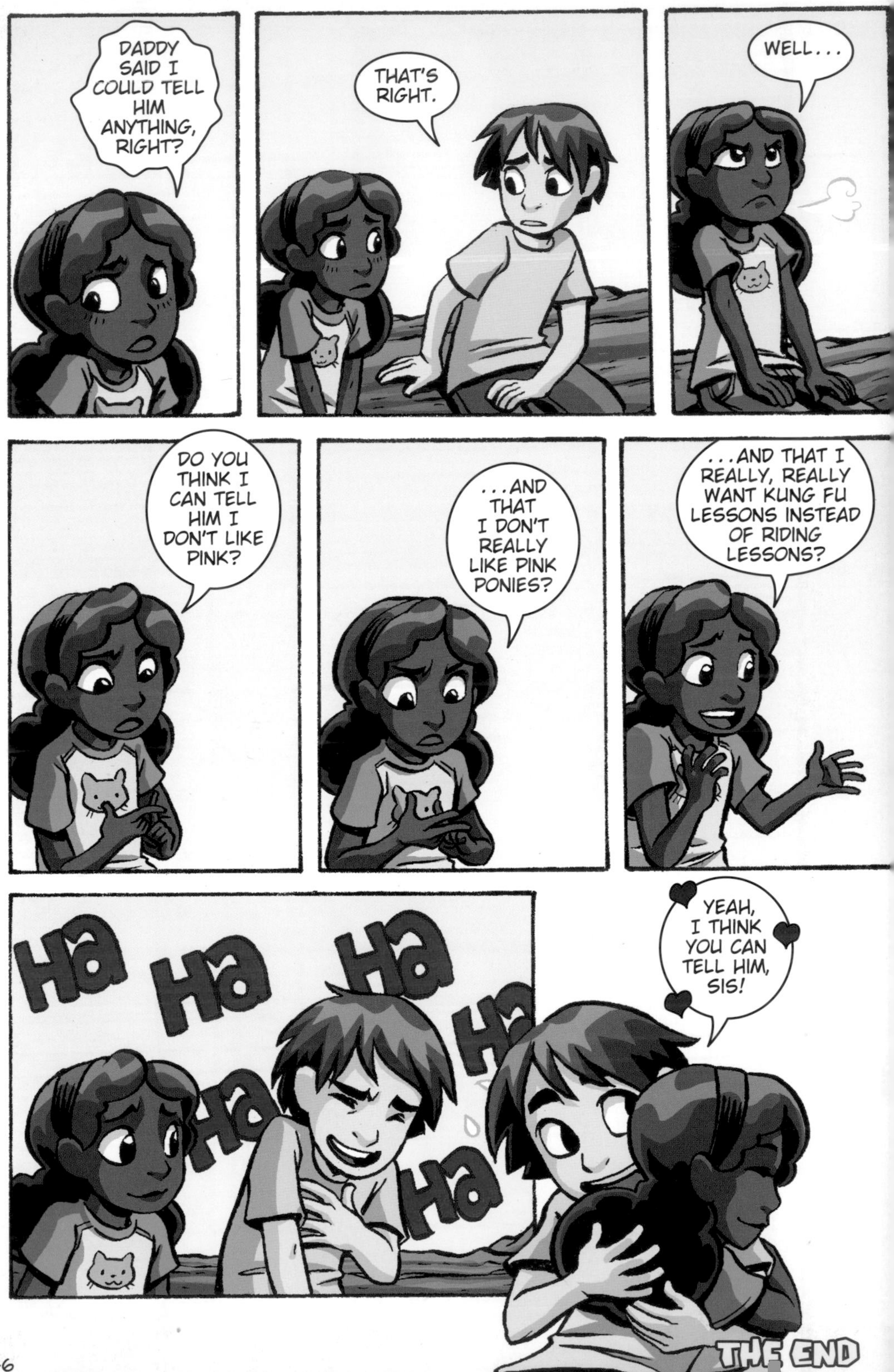
DADDY SAID I COULD TELL HIM ANYTHING, RIGHT?
THAT'S RIGHT.
WELL...
DO YOU THINK I CAN TELL HIM I DON'T LIKE PINK?
...AND THAT I DON'T REALLY LIKE PINK PONIES?
...AND THAT I REALLY, REALLY WANT KUNG FU LESSONS INSTEAD OF RIDING LESSONS?
HA HA HA HA HA HA
YEAH, I THINK YOU CAN TELL HIM, SIS!
THE END

The Author

Melinda Thielbar is a teacher who has written math courses for all ages, from kids to adults. In 2005 Melinda was awarded a VIGRE fellowship at North Carolina State University for PhD candidates "likely to make a strong contribution to education in mathematics." She lives in Raleigh, North Carolina, with her husband, author and video game programmer Richard Dansky, and their two cats.

The Artists

Tintin Pantoja was born in Manila in the Philippines. She received a degree in illustration and cartooning from the School of Visual Arts in New York City and was nominated for the Friends of Lulu "Best Newcomer" award. She was also a finalist in Tokyopop's Rising Stars of Manga 5. Her past books include a graphic novel version for kids of Shakespeare's play *Hamlet*.

Yuko Ota graduated from the Rochester Institute of Technology and lives in Maryland. She has worked as an animator and a lab assistant but is happiest drawing creatures and inventing worlds. She likes strong tea, the smell of new tires, and polydactyl cats (cats with extra toes!). She doesn't have any pets, but she has seven houseplants named Blue, Wolf, Charlene, Charlie, Roberto, Steven, and Doris.

Der-shing Helmer graduated with a degree in biology from UC Berkeley, where she played with snakes and lizards all summer long. She is working toward becoming a biology teacher. When she is not tutoring kids, she likes to create art, especially comics. Her best friends are her two pet geckos (Smeg and Jerry), her king snake (Clarice), and the chinchilla that lives next door.

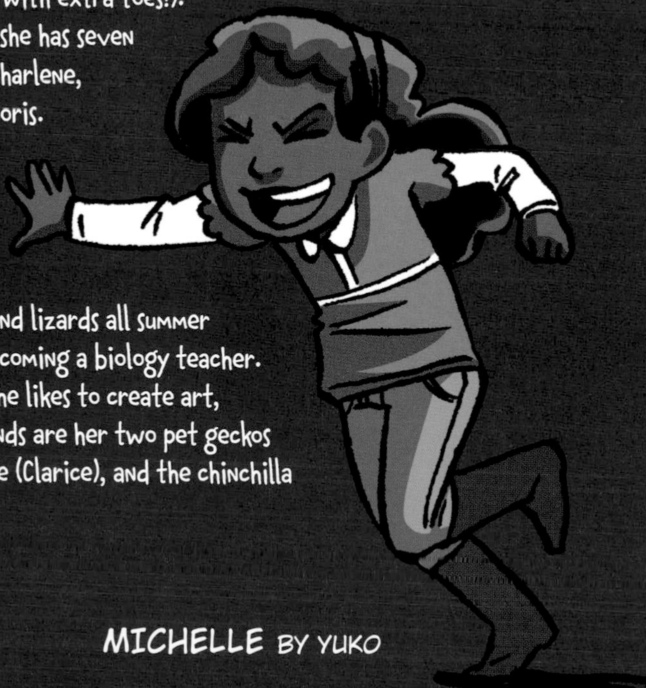

MICHELLE BY YUKO

START READING FROM THE OTHER SIDE OF THE BOOK!

This page would be the first page of a manga from Japan. This is because written Japanese is read from the right side of the page to the left side of the page. English is read from left to right, so this is the last page of this Manga Math Mystery. If you read the end of the book first, you'll spoil the mystery! Turn the book over so you can start on the first page. Then find the clues to the mystery with Sam, Amy, Tom, and Michelle!

MANGA MATH MYSTERIES #4

Is what Adam and Tom overhear true? Is Sifu Faiza is selling the kung fu school? And can they find a way to change her mind in time? All the kids get together to help, but they'll have to figure out a mysterious puzzle about hours, minutes, and temperature to find the unexpected solution in . . .

The Kung Fu Puzzle

MANGA MATH MYSTERIES

- #1 **THE LOST KEY** A Mystery with Whole Numbers
- #2 **THE HUNDRED-DOLLAR ROBBER** A Mystery with Money
- #3 **THE SECRET GHOST** A Mystery with Distance and Measurement
- #4 **THE KUNG FU PUZZLE** A Mystery with Time and Temperature